Presidential Libraries and Museums

AN ILLUSTRATED GUIDE

Presidential Libraries and Museums

AN ILLUSTRATED GUIDE

PAT HYLAND

CONGRESSIONAL QUARTERLY INC.

WASHINGTON, D.C.

Printed and bound in the United States of America.

Typography, book, and cover design by
Kachergis Book Design
Pittsboro, North Carolina

Key to photographs of presidential sites used on the front cover

1	2	1. Roosevelt	2. Truman	
3	4	5	3. Eisenhower	4. Kennedy 5. Johnson
6	7	6. Carter	7. Nixon	
8	9	8. Reagan	9. Ford	

LIBRARY OF CONGRESS CATALOGING–IN–PUBLICATION DATA

Hyland, Pat
     Presidential libraries and museums : an illustrated guide / Pat Hyland.
          p.   cm.
     Includes bibliographical references and index.
     ISBN 0–87187–960–3 (cloth : alk. paper).—ISBN 0–87187–961–1
(paper : alk. paper)
     1. Presidential libraries—United States—Guidebooks. 2. Presidents—
Museums—United States—Guidebooks. I. Title.
CD3029.82.H95   1995
973´.099—dc20   95-17795
                                                     CIP

For my husband, Bud,
my lifetime collaborator in all things,
and for five of our finest projects—
Jenai, Jeff, Todd, Tim, and Brian.

Contents

Preface

━━◉━━

In 1990 I discovered my first presidential library and became one of an estimated one and a half million people who visit the nation's ten presidential libraries and museums each year.

The place was Boston. Arriving at Columbia Point where the John F. Kennedy Library is located, I marveled at the natural beauty of the waterside site and the elegance of the building designed by I. M. Pei. Kennedy's sloop *Victura* appeared ready to sail. I was eager to know more. This had to be a place where history came alive. It did. At the end of my visit I was fascinated and determined to explore the other libraries and their varied collections.

The National Archives and Records Administration oversees nine of the presidential libraries—those dedicated to Herbert Hoover, Franklin Roosevelt, Harry Truman, Dwight Eisenhower, John Kennedy, Lyndon Johnson, Gerald Ford, Jimmy Carter, and Ronald Reagan. The Richard Nixon Library is privately held. This book also describes the Rutherford B. Hayes Library, which is not part of the presidential library system, and the George Bush Library, which is now under construction.

The archives within the libraries are closed to the general public. Permission to use them must be obtained in advance. It is the museums in the presidential libraries that are most frequently visited.

Like the men they have been designed to present, each museum has a personality and style all its own. Exhibits introduce the presidents in a lively and personal way. Their childhoods and families, their distinctive styles and philosophies, are captured through a unique mixture of official records, photos, films, papers, and personal possessions. Materials that can be found nowhere else convey the times in which these men lived and acted as our highest elected officials.

Presidential Libraries and Museums is the guidebook I wish I had when I first began asking questions about these unique national resources. It was assembled with the cooperation of all of the presidential libraries and the National Archives and Records Administration.

Inside these pages you will find a chapter on each museum. Liberally illustrated with photographs, these chapters highlight personal facts about the presidents, such as Hoover's lifelong love of fishing, and landmark legislation, such as the Social Security Act signed by Roosevelt in 1935. The history associated with each man's era, his personal possessions, trivia, presidential symbols, and childhood memories are also included.

Whether you are interested in the museums or in the archives, you will find the information you need: locations, addresses, telephone numbers, museum hours of operation, and library resources and contacts. *Presidential Libraries and Museums* has it all.

Happy touring!

Acknowledgments

⟣⟨◉⟩⟢

For what I have learned about the presidential libraries and associated attractions, I am deeply indebted and grateful to many people:

Sally B. Daubel, director of communications at the Rutherford B. Hayes Presidential Center; Janlyn Ewald, special events coordinator at the Herbert Hoover Presidential Library and Museum; Lynn A. Bassanese, public affairs specialist, and Mark Renovitch, archivist, at the Franklin D. Roosevelt Library; Diane H. Dayson, superintendent, and Franceska Macsali, supervisory park ranger, at the Roosevelt-Vanderbilt National Historic Site; Benedict K. Zobrist, director, George Curtis, assistant director, and Raymond H. Geselbracht, supervisory archivist, at the Harry S. Truman Library; Colleen A. Cearley, public affairs specialist, and Marion Kam, museum registrar, at the Dwight D. Eisenhower Library; Frank Rigg, acting curator for the John F. Kennedy Library, and Shelley Sommer, director of public relations at the John F. Kennedy Library Foundation; Gary A. Yarrington, curator of the Museum at the Lyndon Baines Johnson Library; Kevin Cartwright, assistant director at the Richard Nixon Library and Birthplace; James R. Kratsas, deputy director, and Barbara McGregor Packer, education specialist, at the Gerald R. Ford Museum; William H. McNitt and Kenneth G. Hafeli, archivists at the Gerald R. Ford Library; Donald B. Schewe, director, Martin Elzy, assistant director, and David J. Stanhope, archivist, at the Jimmy Carter Library; Stefanie Salata at the Ronald Reagan Presidential Library; and David Alsobrook, acting director of the Bush Presidential Materials Project, and Rene A. Henry, executive director of university relations, at Texas A&M University.

I would especially like to thank John T. Fawcett, former assistant archivist for the presidential libraries at the National Archives and Records Administration in Washington, D.C. His encouragement and guidance were an immense help to me.

Equally important to this project are my family and friends, especially my husband Bud, who toured eight of the presidential libraries with me, and all of my "cheerleaders," particularly Barry Berkey, Carol Bonham, Lydia Mussulman, and the longtime members of the Springfield Writer's Group: Claude Bache, Charline Barnard, David Boyce, Yereth Knowles, Martha Ruelle, Linda Sultan, and Edgar Werner.

I would like to express my gratitude to Jeanne Ferris, acquisitions editor at Congressional Quarterly Books. Without her, my words and my love of the presidential libraries could not have led to a book. My sincere thanks also go to Barbara de Boinville, who edited the manuscript.

But most of all, I would like to thank the men who have agreed to serve as our presidents. They are heroes—every one.

Presidential Libraries and Museums

AN ILLUSTRATED GUIDE

On November 19, 1939, President Franklin D. Roosevelt prepared the wall of the nation's first presidential library for the cornerstone.

Accompanied by Eleanor Roosevelt and a Secret Service agent, President Roosevelt applies mortar to the cornerstone.

The Presidential Library System

Herbert Hoover—West Branch, Iowa. Franklin D. Roosevelt—Hyde Park, New York. Harry S. Truman—Independence, Missouri. Dwight D. Eisenhower—Abilene, Kansas. John Fitzgerald Kennedy—Boston, Massachusetts. Lyndon Baines Johnson—Austin, Texas. Richard Nixon—Yorba Linda, California. Gerald R. Ford—Ann Arbor and Grand Rapids, Michigan. Jimmy Carter—Atlanta, Georgia. Ronald Reagan—Simi Valley, California. This roll call of men and places signifies the vast network of presidential libraries scattered across the United States. Nine of the ten are administered by the federal government's National Archives and Records Administration (NARA). The single exception is the Richard Nixon Library and Birthplace. It is privately held and does not contain his presidential papers. Next to be added is the George Bush Presidential Library, which will be built at Texas A & M University in College Station, Texas, and is due to open in 1997.

Uniquely American institutions, the presidential libraries are toured by an estimated 1.5 million visitors or more annually. Before being turned over

3

to the federal government, they are privately planned, funded, and constructed. Each contains the official records, films, photographs, and personal papers of a past president and his associates. Each has a museum dedicated to its namesake. In fact, it is the museums within the library system that are most often visited.

Traditionally located on a site chosen for its close connection to the president—a birthplace, a hometown, or an alma mater—every presidential library has a slightly different emphasis (for example, Herbert Hoover, America's role in humanitarian relief activities; Franklin D. Roosevelt, local and naval history; Lyndon Baines Johnson, education, civil rights, and public administration; and Jimmy Carter, human rights).[1] These specialties mirror the interests and achievements of the select group of men who once held our nation's highest office. Distinctive research and educational institutions, each library is an American treasure.

One Man's Vision

Franklin D. Roosevelt could rightly be called the father of the presidential library. Concerned about the volume of papers and other documents being generated by his second term in office, he had a vision that led to the establishment of the first presidential library to be administered by the National Archives.

Presidential papers are now regarded as historical documents, and since 1978 they have been preserved by law. Prior to Roosevelt, however, many presidential collections, by tradition considered the private property of their originators, met ignoble fates. Collections were often poorly treated by the retired presidents or by their descendants. Some were mutilated by autograph collectors or claimed by souvenir hunters. Others were destroyed by widows or ravaged by fire. Most of John Tyler's papers were consumed in the burning of Richmond in 1865. Zachary Taylor's disappeared during the Civil War, carted off by federal troops.[2]

When destruction did not take place, dispersal frequently did. And although efforts to reconstitute past presidents' personal papers have been undertaken, the results have been laborious and expensive. For example, the federal government purchased the major part of George Washington's papers in 1834 for a total sum of $45,000. Similar amounts were raised to obtain the papers of Thomas Jefferson and James Madison.[3] In 1903, several collections held in government custody were transferred to the Library of Congress, and by the late 1930s, the Library held the principal collections of twenty-two presidents. Yet all that could be offered was shelf space, and the collections were fragmented and exceptionally large.

In Franklin Roosevelt's day, there was only one institution that contained the complete body of a specific president's archival materials, the Rutherford B. Hayes Memorial Museum and Library, built in Fremont, Ohio, and dedicated in 1916. In 1982 the expanded facility was renamed the Rutherford B. Hayes Presidential Center. Although not a part of the presidential library system administered by the National Archives, the Center is a valuable resource for presidential scholars and the general public (see Chapter 1).

Apparently convinced that his own papers held the greatest historical value if they remained intact, Roosevelt had the Hayes model investigated. He asked his representatives—among them the man named as the first archivist of the United States, R. D. W. Connor—to examine this facility and to report their findings.

According to all accounts, Roosevelt was impressed with what he heard. On October 21, 1937, he wrote the following to Webb Hayes II, the grandson of President Hayes: "I think it is particularly fitting that this comprehensive collection [at the Hayes Library] should include, besides President Hayes' own library, his correspondence and other papers associated with his public life—a veritable gold mine for historical scholars."[4]

This was not Roosevelt's only involvement, however. A very hands-on individual, he drew a sketch, dated April 12, 1937, that shows his proposed library building placed on his Hyde Park estate very close to the site ultimately chosen. He also sought the opinions of leaders in business and education, including Helen Taft Manning, dean of Bryn Mawr College. She was an outstanding historian and the daughter of our twenty-seventh president, William Howard Taft.

Having completed his investigation, Roosevelt made a decision. On December 10, 1938, he called a White House press conference and announced his intention to create a library:

For the past two years I have been considering more and more the final disposal of what amounts to probably the largest collection of original source material of almost anybody over the last quarter of a century and it is very voluminous. It includes all of my papers when I was in the State Senate, all of my personal papers when I was in the Navy Department, including the war period. It includes the Vice Presidential Campaign of 1920 and the Convention of 1924, the Convention of 1928, the four years as Governor and I have, up in Albany, sixty packing cases full of those papers of the Governorship. It includes the Campaigns of 1928 and 1930, the Presidential Campaigns of 1932 and 1936, plus all the Presidential papers and the file I operate.

The amount of material that I have is so infinitely larger than that of any previous President that it creates a new problem. As I remember it, when we came in here we were told that President Hoover, his mail averaged about four hundred letters a day. My mail has averaged, as you know, about four thousand letters a day. Well, there is all the difference in the world.[5]

After fully describing the problem as he saw it, Roosevelt also delivered the solution. He would give his collections to the federal government, but place them at Hyde Park where he could have a hand in cataloging them. Private funds would be raised for a separate, fireproof building on the Roosevelt family estate. This building would eventually be deeded over to and be maintained by the federal government. Operated for the benefit of the American public, the facility would become the responsibility of the archivist of the United States.

Roosevelt explained in the speech that the purpose was to keep his papers "whole and intact in their original condition, available to the scholars of the future in one definite locality."[6] He envisioned his library as a manuscript repository as well as a historical museum—two parts of the whole that represented his career, his presidency and the era in which he lived. The papers and other historical materials in the Library reflect Roosevelt's image of himself as a man as well as the president of the United States.

Without the actions of Presidents Truman and Eisenhower, the Roosevelt Presidential Library might have become, like the Hayes Museum and Library, a stand alone institution. Both men decided to follow the Roosevelt model. Because of them, Congress passed the Presidential Libraries Act of 1955. Under its terms, the National Archives has the authority to accept papers, artifacts, lands, and buildings in connection with the establishment of presidential libraries. The Harry S. Truman Library was formally dedicated and opened to the public in 1957. The Dwight D. Eisenhower and the Herbert Hoover libraries followed in 1962. Since that time a library has been opened for each succeeding president.

Library Administration

Presidential papers normally became government property through gift of deed until 1978. Then, as a result of the Watergate scandal and former president Nixon's refusal to turn certain presidential papers over to the government, Congress passed the Presidential Records Act of 1978. This gave ownership of the presidential records of Ronald Reagan and his successors to the United States. Although there are some narrowly defined exceptions related to personal and political activities, a document filed in the White House now remains in the custody of the National Archives.

The National Archives and Records Administration has been an independent agency since 1984. It was preceded by the National Archives Establishment, founded in 1934, and the National Archives and Records Service (NARS), part of the General Services Administration from 1949 to 1984. The Office of Presidential Libraries was created within NARS in 1964, and twenty years later became part of the National Archives and Records Administration. The Office of the Presidential Libraries is now headed by the assistant archivist for the presidential libraries. Before 1964 all such duties were attended to by the archivist of the United States.[7]

The Office of the Presidential Libraries oversees the acquisition, preservation, and use of historical materials appropriate for deposit in presidential libraries. It also serves as a liaison with the incumbent administration and with the officials of former administrations concerning the organization and storage of presidential papers and other historical materials.[8]

This system preserves presidential records and makes them available for research, generally six to seven years after a president's term of office ends. Researchers and scholars request permission to work with presidential collections as they become available.

Future of the Presidential Library System

Presidential libraries evolve, going through three distinct stages, writes Don W. Wilson, archivist of the United States from 1987 to 1993. During the first stage, lasting approximately ten years, the museum is developed as its staff catalogs and surveys artifacts. Archivists devote their time to the processing of substantive, nonclassified files. The library moves from temporary to permanent quarters. The library's managers solicit collections and seek to raise community interest. Museum visitation levels are high for the first three to five years and then level off.

The second stage, lasting fifteen to twenty years, is one of professional and research use. The workload of the archivists is high as they process more complex collections as well as collections that may contain numbers of classified documents. The demands of soliciting and accessioning diminish. The museum staff devotes its energies to maintaining local and regional community interest. Scholarly conferences and educational programs often become fully established during this phase.

The third and last stage, which Wilson refers to as nostalgia, is a period of recollection and reexamination of the president and an expanded focus on his times. Most archival collections have already been processed, and those that remain unprocessed are usually of lesser interest to scholars. The level of research activity subsides. In order to become an invaluable community resource rather than an archival warehouse, many mature libraries reach out to nonacademic and nontraditional audiences.[9]

Presidential libraries offer new exhibits, lectures, scholarly programs, conferences, and symposia in an attempt to create a fresh public awareness of past presidents, their decisions, and their duties while in office. The importance of this mission was affirmed by Franklin D. Roosevelt at the dedication of the first presidential library:

It seems to me that the dedication of a library is in itself an act of faith, to bring together the records of the past and to house them in buildings where they will be preserved for the use of men and women in the future. A nation must believe in— in three things.

It must believe in the past.
It must believe in the future.
It must, above all, believe in the capacity of its own people so to learn from the past that they can gain in judgement in creating their own future.[10]

For more than half a century, presidential libraries have built upon Roosevelt's words and fostered these beliefs.

Notes

1. Frank L. Schick with Renee Schick and Mark Carroll, Foreword by President Gerald R. Ford, *Records of the Presidency: Presidential Papers and Libraries from Washington to Reagan* (Phoenix, Ariz.: Oryx Press, 1989), 12.

2. Don W. Wilson, "Presidential Libraries: Developing to Maturity," *Presidential Studies Quarterly* 21, no. 4 (Fall 1991): 772.

3. Herman Kahn, director of the Franklin D. Roosevelt Library, "The Presidential Library: A New Institution," March 1958.

4. Wilson, "Presidential Libraries," 771.

5. William R. Emerson, director of the Franklin D. Roosevelt Library, *Materials Relevant to the Founding of the Franklin D. Roosevelt Library,* Exhibit VI, transcript of the president's press conference announcing his plan to build the Roosevelt Library.

6. Donald R. McCoy, "The Beginnings of the Franklin D. Roosevelt Library," reprinted from *Prologue: The Journal of the National Archives* (Fall 1975).

7. "National Archives and Records Administration," *Funk & Wagnalls New Encyclopedia,* vol. 18 (New York: Funk & Wagnalls L.P., 1987), 275.

8. Schick, *Records of the Presidency,* 11.

9. Wilson, "Presidential Libraries," 775.

10. William R. Emerson, *Materials,* Exhibit IX, Speech of the president, dedication of the Franklin D. Roosevelt Library, June 30, 1941.

Inside the Museums

CHAPTER 1

Rutherford B. Hayes

MEMORIAL MUSEUM AND LIBRARY OPENED:

MAY 30, 1916, FREMONT, OHIO

Rutherford B. Hayes, a Republican, was America's nineteenth president.

He served one term (1877–1881).

WHEN THE Rutherford B. Hayes Memorial Museum and Library opened to the public on May 30, 1916, it was the first institution of its kind in the United States. This building with a dual function was founded by President Hayes's son Webb C. Hayes I and the Ohio Historical Society to honor the president's memory and to house his personal and political papers and the artifacts of his administration. President Franklin D. Roosevelt used the Hayes Memorial as a model for his own library and described its collection in a letter to Webb Hayes II, the grandson of President Hayes, as a "veritable gold mine for historical scholars."[1]

In 1982 the expanded facility was renamed the Rutherford B. Hayes Presidential Center. Although it is not a part of the presidential library system administered by the National Archives, the Center is a valuable resource for presidential scholars and the general public. It is located on a twenty-five-acre wooded estate named Spiegel Grove.

A visitor to the Center today will find the museum and library in a classically designed two-story building with a four-pillared entryway; President and Mrs. Hayes's home, a thirty-three-room mansion opened to the public in 1966; Dillon House, a nineteenth-century Victorian building that now serves as a guesthouse and meeting center; and the tombs of the president and his wife. Lucy Webb Hayes died in 1889. The president was buried beside her when he died at Spiegel Grove on January 17, 1893, at the age of seventy.

The Presidential Center's museum contains more than 10,000 objects that belonged to the president, his family, and his administration. In 1852 he married his childhood sweetheart, Lucy Webb Hayes, who bore him eight children. Much of his administration was devoted to ending Reconstruction in the South and to preserving nationalism. Displays cover Hayes's distin-

The Rutherford B. Hayes Presidential Center Museum/Library building at Spiegel Grove contains material that reflects the life and diverse interests of President Hayes and his period of history. It is visited by some 40,000 individuals annually.

guished career before he became president: city solicitor in Cincinnati (1858), major general of volunteers in the Civil War (1865), member of the U.S. House of Representatives (1865–1867), and governor of Ohio elected three times (1867, 1869, 1875). Two of the favorite exhibits are a collection of military equipment (including weapons used by General Hayes during the Civil War) and the ornate doll houses that belonged to the president's daughter Fanny.

The Presidential Center's library currently holds more than 1 million

The Rutherford B. Hayes home at Spiegel Grove in Fremont, Ohio, is open to the public 362 days a year. The 25-acre wooded estate includes gardens, a carriage house, and more than a mile of historic hiking trails.

manuscripts and nearly 100,000 books, pamphlets, and other material relating to President Hayes's life, administration, and the Gilded Age period (circa 1860–1917) in which he lived. Materials concerning genealogy and local Ohio history reflect President Hayes's special interests in these topics. In addition, there are collections on topics as diverse as Great Lakes shipping, nineteenth-century prison reform (a special interest of President Hayes), and Abraham Lincoln.

The Hayes's home, constructed in three stages between 1859 and 1889, contains the original furnishings and many beautiful antiques that belonged to the president and his family.[2]

The Hayes Presidential Center is open Monday through Saturday from 9:00 A.M. to 5:00 P.M. and Sundays from noon to 5:00 P.M. every day except Thanksgiving, Christmas, and New Year's Day. The Center is located at Spiegel Grove, 1337 Hayes Avenue in Fremont, Ohio 43420. Admission fee for those six years and older. For additional information, telephone (419) 332-2081.

NOTES

1. Don W. Wilson, "Presidential Libraries: Developing to Maturity," *Presidential Studies Quarterly* 21, no. 4 (Fall 1991): 771.

2. For more information see the one-page brochure entitled *The Rutherford B. Hayes Presidential Center (Affiliated with the Ohio Historical Society) Summary Background and Programs* and the four-color brochure entitled *Rutherford B. Hayes Presidential Center.* Both are published by the Center.

CHAPTER 2

Herbert Hoover

LIBRARY DEDICATED: AUGUST 10, 1962

WEST BRANCH, IOWA

Herbert Hoover, a Republican, became president on March 4, 1929,

and served one term (1929–1933).

ALTHOUGH Herbert Hoover preceded Franklin D. Roosevelt, Harry S. Truman, and Dwight D. Eisenhower as president, his presidential library was not dedicated until theirs were already established. This seems appropriate. Generally ignored by the Roosevelt administration, Hoover was called upon by President Truman to head two post–World War II global relief missions and to direct a plan to reorganize the executive branch of the federal government—the so-called Hoover Commission. President Eisenhower later asked the former president to head a second Hoover Commission.

When the Herbert Hoover Presidential Library was dedicated on August 10, 1962, Hoover's eighty-eighth birthday, former president Truman was there. Hoover, Truman said, "did a job for me that nobody else in the world could have done. He kept millions of people from starving to death after the Second World War just as he did after the first World War. . . . He did a most wonderful job of keeping these people from starving. What more can a man do?"[1]

At the dedication ceremony Hoover explained why his presidential library is located in West Branch.

I was taken from this village to the Far West 78 years ago. The only material assets which I had were two dimes in my pocket, the suit of clothes that I wore and I had some extra underpinnings provided by loving aunts. But I carried from here something much more precious.

I had a stern grounding of religious faith.

I carried with me recollections of a joyous childhood.

And I carried with me the family disciplines of hard work.[2]

The Herbert Hoover Presidential Library, owned and operated by the National Archives and Records Administration, is located on the Herbert Hoover National Historic Site, 178 acres administered by the National Park Service. Seventy-six acres are tall-grass prairie located a few hundred feet south of the Library. Additional attractions on the site include President Hoover's birthplace, a reconstruction of his father's blacksmith shop, the Quaker meetinghouse where Hoover worshiped as a child, a schoolhouse, and the gravesite where Hoover and his wife are buried.

As a result of a $6.5 million renovation and expansion project completed in 1992, the Herbert Hoover Library is one of the newest libraries in the system. The one-story, neo-colonial, limestone building, expanded from 32,000 to 43,000 square feet, was rededicated by former president Ronald Reagan on August 8, 1992. Its updated exhibit galleries are filled with interactive displays and state-of-the-art push-button exhibits.

Seated inside a newly renovated 178-seat auditorium, you view a twenty-two-minute biographical film composed of still photos, period documentaries, and battle footage from World War I. You learn that before he became president, Hoover was a successful mining engineer and businessman who began a life of public service in 1914. After heading the Commission for Relief in Belgium, he was U.S. food administrator from 1917 to 1919 and secretary of commerce from 1921 to 1928 under Presidents Calvin Coolidge and Warren G. Harding.

Tours begin in a rotunda area where a sixteen-foot red granite map of the world is located. During his fifty years of humanitarian service, Herbert Hoover was responsible for providing food relief in fifty-seven countries. Each of these countries is emblazoned by a symbolic brass sheaf of wheat. Mounted on the rotunda wall are two eight-foot, glass-etched portraits of Hoover at the beginning and near the end of his public career.

Exiting the rotunda, you enter the first of six permanent galleries, "Years of Adventure," and learn about the earliest influences on this man. The gallery starts with the image of a barefoot five-year old. "I carry the brand of

The Herbert Hoover Library contains a newly expanded museum that enables visitors to gain insight into the many sides of Iowa's only president.

Iowa," Hoover said, recalling the day he stepped on a hot iron in his father's blacksmith shop.[3] Hoover's early history is quickly recounted: a Quaker upbringing, the loss of both parents by the age of ten, and a train ride to Oregon where Hoover was raised by his Quaker uncle, John Minthorn.

In the fall of 1891, Hoover entered the new Leland Stanford Junior University at Palo Alto, California, to study geology. He earned a degree and met his bride to be, Miss Lou Henry. Jobs in exotic places followed. One display takes you to the Australian outback where Hoover started his mining career. It is easy to imagine it exactly as he described it, "a land of red dust, black flies and white heat."[4]

Hoover's life story begins in gallery one where lifelike figures depict him as a boy and in a rugged Australian mining camp.

A second display takes you to the living room in China of the newly married couple. It is the summer of 1899 and the Boxer Rebellion has broken out, keeping the couple trapped within the foreign quarters of Tientsin for ten weeks. Of their rescue the future president said: "I do not remember a more satisfying musical performance than the bugles of the American Marines entering the settlement playing 'There'll Be a Hot Time in the Old Town Tonight.'" [5]

Then it's on to the second gallery, "The Great Humanitarian." With World War I about to begin, Hoover, who was then in London, received a request from the U.S. ambassador to Britain, Walter Hines Page, to bring 120,000 Americans home from Europe. "I did not realize it at the moment, but on August 3, 1914, my engineering career was over forever. I was on the slippery road of public life," he said.[6]

Visitors enter a World War I Belgian relief warehouse and weave around sacks of flour and wooden food crates. Sitting among these lifesaving supplies, you hear survivors of the Great War recalling their experiences, telling how America (and Hoover) first came to their rescue.

Belgium was not Hoover's only concern. Part of one museum script explains that "Hoover's European Children's Fund—forerunner of CARE— alone helped six million victims of war. Overall it has been estimated that Hoover's relief efforts during and immediately after World War I rescued between 15 and 20 million children."[7]

Hoover's accomplishments in Europe did not pass unnoticed back in the United States. President Woodrow Wilson asked Hoover to become director of the new U.S. Food Administration, and he complied, doing such an outstanding job that a 1920 *New York Times* newspaper poll ranked him among the ten greatest living Americans.

In the third gallery, "The Roaring Twenties," this decade is recreated through period music and photos. Among other facts, you are reminded that it is the era of Prohibition. Charles Lindbergh makes his solo flight across the Atlantic. John Scopes is tried and convicted for teaching evolution in a Tennessee school. Life expectancy rises.

Also in this gallery is "The Wonder Boy" display, a giant three-dimensional montage of Hoover's accomplishments as secretary of commerce and "undersecretary of everything else." You learn that Hoover wrote the first highway safety codes and, in 1927, participated in the first demonstration of television. An added attraction is the Hoover Quote Game. History buffs can push buttons to match quotes to famous persons ranging from Helen Keller to Karl Marx.[8]

With another presidential campaign on the horizon, "Who but Hoover?" the nation asks. In the fourth gallery, "The Logical Candidate," visitors stand on a replica of Hoover's inaugural platform on March 4, 1929, and see a multiscreen video of America before the Crash. Hoover has made his first months in office a "whirlwind of reform." After Wall Street's Black Tuesday and the worsening Great Depression, Hoover moves "From Hero to Scapegoat," the title of one display in the fourth gallery. By way of introduction a script reads: "No American president entered office with greater expectations, or left with more bitter disappointments than Hoover did."[9]

In spite of Hoover's best efforts, the Depression continues, and he loses his reelection bid to Franklin D. Roosevelt. Banks in the states of New York and Illinois falter. When banking operations in both states are suspended, Hoover laments: "We are at the end of our string. There is nothing more we can do."[10] Visitors are invited to register by computer their opinion of Hoover's handling of events during his presidential term (1929–1933).

Leaving these years in the White House, visitors make the acquaintance of "An Uncommon Woman" in the fifth gallery. Like her husband, Lou Henry Hoover loved the outdoors, traveled widely, and was engaged in public service. She was also one of the first women in America to earn a geology degree. She helped design Camp Rapidan, the president's retreat 100 miles from Washington, D.C., in Virginia's Shenandoah Mountains. Peeking inside the cabin windows, visitors catch a glimpse of home movies actually taken by Mrs. Hoover.

Hoover's long postpresidential career is recounted in the last gallery, "Years of Struggle and Accomplishment." Two rooms from Suite 31-A in New

As former president, Hoover lived simply in Suite 31-A in New York's elegant Waldorf Towers. Its re-created living room is found in the museum's last gallery.

York's elegant Waldorf Towers are re-created, complete with many original furnishings. It was here that Hoover wrote books and articles and supported his many causes, including the Boys Club of America. He died at the Waldorf Towers on October 20, 1964, at the age of ninety.

Visitors learn how the nation mourned his loss:

Following ceremonies in New York and Washington, a C-30 Hercules aircraft bearing the body of Iowa's only president touched down in Cedar Rapids on Sunday,

October 25. Thousands of people lined the thirty three mile route to West Branch, where a crowd estimated at 75,000 stood silently on a warm Indian Summer afternoon.... Today America's 31st president lies beneath a slab of Vermont marble within sight of the tiny cottage where his life began. In a final demonstration of Quaker simplicity there is no presidential seal, no inscription of any kind, just the name Herbert Hoover and the dates 1874–1964.[11]

The final image in the gallery is a lifelike statue of the former president standing in a mountain brook, doing what he loved best, fishing. "Fishing is the chance to wash one's soul with pure air, with the rush of the brook, or with the shimmer of sun on the blue water," Hoover once wrote. "It brings meekness and inspiration from the decency of nature, charity toward tackle makers, patience toward fish, a mockery of profit and egos, a quieting of hate, a rejoicing that you do not have to decide a darned thing until next week. And it is discipline in the equality of men, for all men are equal before fish."[12]

Birthplace Cottage

This 14-by-20-foot cottage (two rooms with a shed at the rear) was built by Herbert Hoover's father, Jesse, and grandfather, Eli, in 1871. It stands on its original site at the corner of Downey and Penn streets. Herbert, the second of three children, was born here on August 10, 1874. Five years later Jesse sold the cottage and his blacksmith shop and moved his family into a large dwelling farther south on Downey Street. By 1885 both parents had died, and Hoover went to live in Newberg, Oregon, with his uncle, Dr. John Minthorn. Hoover did not visit West Branch again until 1923. Five years later he opened his midwestern campaign for the presidency in West Branch.

In 1935 the Hoover family acquired the Birthplace Cottage, which had changed hands several times. It was restored to its 1874 appearance under the direction of Lou Henry Hoover and furnished as much as possible with original pieces. Of his Iowa background, Hoover recalled on November 10,

With his life-long passion for fishing, this late-in-life figure of Hoover shows him where he claimed to be happiest, fishing in a trout stream.

1927, "I prefer to think of Iowa as I saw it through the eyes of a ten-year old boy—and the eyes of all ten-year old Iowa boys are or should be filled with the wonders of Iowa's streams and woods, of the mystery of growing crops. His days should be filled with adventure and great undertakings, with participation in good and comforting things." [13]

Blacksmith Shop

The Blacksmith Shop, northwest of the cottage, is similar to the one operated by Herbert Hoover's father from 1871 to 1879. It is equipped with tools of the day, and visitors learn that they were used to provide for the needs of the surrounding farm community.

Friends' Meetinghouse

The Friends' Meetinghouse, a large well-lit building, was constructed by the Society of Friends (or Quakers) in 1857. As a child Herbert Hoover worshiped here with his family. Services consisted of unprogrammed, silent meditation interspersed with spiritual insights and messages. His mother, Hulda Hoover, often spoke. The Meetinghouse originally stood about two blocks from this site.

Schoolhouse

The one-story schoolhouse, originally used as a meetinghouse, was built at a cost of $800 in 1853. It was moved from its original one-acre location at Downey and Main streets, relocated several more times, and then placed here in 1971.

Gravesite

Known as the Overlook, the Gravesite contains a circular setting for the plain white marble stones marking the graves of Herbert Hoover and his wife, Lou Henry Hoover. Both are shielded from the prairie wind by a simple stand of cypress.

The Herbert Hoover National Historic Site, which includes the Presidential Library, is located in West Branch, Iowa. The National Park Service visitor center is on Parkside Drive and Main Street, one-half mile north from Exit 254 off Interstate 80. The park's historic buildings and the library-museum are open daily except Thanksgiving, Christmas, and New Year's Day.

Hours are usually 9:00 A.M. to 5:00 P.M., but they increase during the summer season. One fee for those sixteen years and older covers admission to all attractions. Library information: (319) 643-5301.

NOTES

1. Quoted in a one-page sheet on the dedication supplied by the staff of the Herbert Hoover Library.

2. Ibid.

3. Richard Norton Smith, Maureen H. Harding, and Timothy Walch, *Herbert Hoover Library & Museum: A Guide to the Exhibit Galleries* (West Branch, Iowa: Herbert Hoover Library and Museum, 1993).

4. "Ronald Reagan to Dedicate New Hoover Library-Museum August 8," press release, Hoover Presidential Library Association, Inc., 1992.

5. Smith, Harding, and Walch, *Herbert Hoover*, 14.

6. Ibid., 16.

7. Ibid., 18.

8. Rebecca Christian, "Revisiting Herbert Hoover," *Home and Away*, American Automobile Association of America (AAA) Iowa, January/February 1993, 1A-3A.

9. Smith, Harding, and Walch, *Herbert Hoover*, 56.

10. Ibid., 60.

11. Ibid., 74.

12. Richard Norton Smith, *An Uncommon Man: The Triumph of Herbert Hoover* (New York: Simon and Schuster, 1984), 403–404.

13. *Herbert Hoover: Official Map and Guide, National Historic Site, Iowa,* National Park Service, U.S. Department of the Interior.

CHAPTER 3

Franklin D. Roosevelt

LIBRARY DEDICATED: JUNE 30, 1941

HYDE PARK, NEW YORK

Franklin D. Roosevelt, a Democrat, was elected to an

unprecedented four terms (1933–1937, 1937–1941, 1941–1945, 1945–1949)

as president. He unexpectedly died in office on April 12, 1945,

eighty-three days into his fourth term.

P ASS A WOODEN sheep fence and head up the drive toward the library's gate house. You can almost see the scene Franklin D. Roosevelt described on November 19, 1939, when he laid the Library's cornerstone:

Half a century ago a small boy took especial delight in climbing an old tree, now unhappily gone, to pick and eat ripe Seckel pears. That was one hundred feet to the west of where we now stand. Just to the north he used to lie flat between the strawberry rows and eat sun-warmed strawberries. In the Spring of the year, in hip rubber boots, he sailed his first toy boats in the surface water formed by the melting snows. In the Summer, with his dogs, he dug into the woodchuck holes of this same field. The descendants of those same woodchucks still inhabit the field, and I hope they will continue to do so for all time.[1]

Franklin D. Roosevelt's love of the outdoors began at an early age. An only child, he learned to ride and sail with his father. Astride his pony, he accompanies his father on horseback. His mother, Sara, poses in the foreground with a dog.

With its emphasis on the history of his times, the Franklin D. Roosevelt Library set a pattern for future presidents.

With these boyhood memories, it is easy to understand why Roosevelt wanted his library established at Hyde Park. In keeping with the architectural style of the surrounding area, the building is a one-story, Dutch colonial of natural field stone with a high-pitched roof. It was turned over to the U.S. government on July 4, 1940, and opened to the public on June 30, 1941.

Step up the walk and past a large bust of Roosevelt before entering the library's museum, which was completed in 1972 when two wings in honor of Mrs. Roosevelt were added. Almost immediately you discover Roosevelt's White House desk from the Oval Office as it must have looked during his twelve years as president. Its surface is covered with books, vases, nautical items, a telephone, and clusters of donkeys and elephants, symbols of the

Democratic and Republican parties. This was a complex man who viewed himself as the president of all the people. You can almost hear him saying: "I, Franklin Delano Roosevelt, do solemnly swear that I will faithfully execute the Office of President of United States and will to the best of my ability, preserve, protect, and defend, the Constitution of the United States, so help me God."

On March 4, 1933, when Roosevelt took office, the Great Depression was in its fourth year. Twenty-five percent of the nation's work force was unemployed. Roosevelt moved the presidency from a passive to an active role in this crisis. "This nation asks for action, and action now," promised Roo-

Franklin Roosevelt still holds the record for the most press conferences. He held 998 news conferences, averaging 6.9 a month during his twelve-year presidency.

Although FDR's staff remained small and unstructured, the role of Harry Hopkins, special assistant to the president, resembled that of today's chief of staff.

sevelt. His now-famous First One Hundred Days in office were characterized by sixteen actions, beginning with Roosevelt's declaration of the National Bank Holiday on March 4, 1933, and ending with the Railroad Coordination Act on June 16, 1933.

The museum's Presidential Gallery shows how Roosevelt interpreted and executed the duties of his office from the First One Hundred Days to the threshold of victory in World War II. His activist philosophy is summed up in this quote by him regarding the New Deal: "Above all, try something."

During World War II FDR made a series of trips overseas to confer with allied leaders about military strategy and the composition of the postwar world. In February 1945 Roosevelt conferred with Winston Churchill and Joseph Stalin at Yalta in the Crimea.

During Roosevelt's presidency, he tried many things. He created the Tennessee Valley Authority in 1933 to benefit one of the nation's most impoverished areas, signed the Social Security Act of 1935 into law, and established America's pre-World War II and wartime policies. Then in February of 1945, two months before his death, he met at Yalta in the Soviet Union with British prime minister Winston Churchill and Soviet premier Joseph Stalin to work out postwar plans. Faced with issues, both domestic and foreign, he always tried something.

Seated at his desk, President Roosevelt spoke to the nation by radio, becoming famous for his "fireside chats."

It is a short walk from the Presidential Gallery to the study, an elegantly appointed room where Roosevelt received visitors. Just outside its door is a salute to Fala, Roosevelt's famous Scottie dog. His full name was "Murray, the Outlaw of Falahill," and he spent four years at the White House. In 1943 a movie was made about Fala by MGM and presented to the president by Herbert Morgan.

Inside the study Roosevelt broadcast four of his wartime "fireside chats."

Here, too, he worked on his books, stamps, and papers. Everything reflects his personal tastes and interests. At the time of his death, 1,200,000 stamps from his extensive collection were sold for $228,000. There were no famous rarities, but the collection reflects the president's fascination with almost every human endeavor.

Then it is time to step back. Who was this man before he became president of the United States? Browsing through the gallery titled Roosevelt's "First Fifty Years" (1892–1932), it is easy to believe that he and his family never threw anything away. On display are locks of baby hair, Roosevelt's christening gown, books he read as a child, his first pony saddle, a school microscope, and the cane he used after he was stricken with polio in 1921.[2] There is even a hobby horse that he named "Mexico," because his parents were traveling in that country at the time he received the gift from his Delano grandparents.

Roosevelt's education, first at Groton, then at Harvard, from which he graduated in 1904, is also chronicled in the "First Fifty Years" exhibit. Roosevelt was editor-in-chief of the *Harvard Crimson,* and a copy of this daily newspaper is on display. His love of winter sports and his proposal to his fifth cousin once removed, Eleanor, during his last year at Harvard are also noted. In addition the exhibit traces his distinguished political career prior to the presidency: New York State senator (1910–1913), assistant secretary of the navy (1913–1920), unsuccessful vice-presidential candidate (1920), and two-term governor of New York (1929–1933).

Descend to the museum's lower level and you discover an exhibit centered on one of Roosevelt's life-long passions, the sea. The ship models, artworks, letters, logs, and documents, some dating back to 1775, are from the president's collections. They depict America's naval and maritime history during the age of sail.

Near this exhibit titled "America on the Seas" is one of the museum's most popular displays, Roosevelt's car. It is a 1936 Ford Phaeton equipped with special hand controls for the president, whose legs were paralyzed. Along with a detailed description of how those controls could be operated is a behind-the-wheel photograph of a buoyant Roosevelt. The car had been driven 19,146 miles when it was given to the museum by Mrs. Roosevelt in 1946.

The Eleanor Roosevelt Gallery

Added to the original library building in 1972, the Eleanor Roosevelt Gallery honors Mrs. Roosevelt and her accomplishments. The displays trace her life from child, to wife, to mother, to First Lady of the Land, to First Lady of the World, as she became known after her husband's death. Her extensive travels are captured in a *New Yorker* cartoon dated June 3, 1933. A working coal miner comments: "For gosh sakes, here comes Mrs. Roosevelt." She was likely to turn up almost anywhere.

Eleanor Roosevelt became active in Democratic Party politics after her husband was stricken with poliomyelitis in 1921. This was her way of keeping his political career alive. Her political assistance continued after he was elected president in 1932.

Remembered for many things, Mrs. Roosevelt sponsored an experiment at Arthurdale, West Virginia, designed to bring small-scale manufacturing to impoverished coal miners; resigned from the Daughters of the American Revolution when they refused black singer Marian Anderson use of their facilities; visited American soldiers around the world during World War II; and served as a U.S. delegate to the United Nations from 1945 to 1953. During those years she was chairperson of the commission that drafted the Universal Declaration of Human Rights. During the 1950s, she strongly supported Democratic Party leader Adlai Stevenson.

The Franklin D. Roosevelt National Historic Site

Located on the grounds just behind the Franklin D. Roosevelt Library
and Museum is the lifetime home of our thirty-second president. The only
child of James and Sara Roosevelt, he was born here on January 30, 1882.

The central part of the building, the oldest section, dates back to the early
1800s. When James Roosevelt purchased the house in 1867, it had a clapboard exterior. Since then the main house has undergone many renovations
and additions. In 1915 the clapboards were removed from the central portion
and covered with stucco. A front porch with a sweeping balustrade and small
colonnaded portico was added, as well as two-story wings at each end. The
roof was also raised to add a third floor to the structure.

A tour of the Roosevelt family home enhances the visitor's understanding of the Roosevelts'
comfortable and gracious lifestyle at Hyde Park.

In 1905 Roosevelt brought his bride Eleanor to live at Hyde Park. Later, after they established a home of their own, they and their five children were frequent visitors. Throughout his long political career, Roosevelt remained connected to this place. He spent much of his time here during the first years of his struggle with polio, and he returned as often as possible during his terms as governor of New York and president of the United States.

"He particularly admired the beautiful view, as did everyone, from the terrace at the southern end of the house," wrote Roosevelt's former secretary of labor, Frances Perkins, in her memoir *The Roosevelt I Knew*.

One stepped out long French windows from the living-room-library and onto a green lawn. Many times in summer, when I would be told that "the family was on the lawn," I approached through the library and saw through the open door an unforgettable picture: Mrs. Sara Roosevelt in a soft, summery dress with ruffles, her hair charmingly curled, sitting in a wicker chair and reading; Mrs. Roosevelt, in a white dress and white tennis shoes with a velvet band around her head to keep the hair from blowing, sitting with her long-legged, graceful posture in a low chair and knitting, always knitting; Roosevelt looking off down the river at the view he admired, with a book, often unopened, in one hand, and a walking stick in the other; dogs playing near by, and children romping a little further down the lawn. The scene was like a Currier and Ives print of Life along the Hudson.[3]

The house has seen many historic moments. In the president's first floor office (his "summer White House") Roosevelt and Churchill signed an agreement on June 20, 1942, that resulted in the building of the world's first atomic bomb. The office was also used by the president on November 6, 1944, when he broadcast his last campaign speech that led to his fourth term. Although visitors are not allowed to enter this room, it can be viewed from outside and a recording of Roosevelt's words in that speech can be heard.

Entering the home's Main Hall, a visitor becomes immediately aware of the family's interests and comfortable way of life. A few large pieces of furniture dominate this room, and the walls are covered with pictures, mostly naval prints. Directly to the left of the entranceway stands a massive oak wardrobe, and immediately before the door, an eighteenth century grandfather clock. James and Sara Roosevelt purchased these pieces in the Netherlands in 1881.

Against the wall, just to the left of the clock, stands a large sideboard that James Roosevelt bought in Italy in 1869. In the southeast corner of the hall is a life-size bronze statue of Franklin D. Roosevelt at the age of twenty-nine. It was done by Prince Paul Troubetzkey in 1911. Behind the statue is a wall case that holds many birds Roosevelt collected when he was eleven years old.

The south hallway leads past the "Snuggery," Sara Delano Roosevelt's writing and sitting room, to the living room, which occupies the lower floor of the south wing. It is easy to picture the family playing, reading, and entertaining in this spacious room with two fireplaces.

Over the fireplace on the left side of the living room hangs Gilbert Stuart's portrait of Issac Roosevelt, the president's great-great-great grandfather, who was active in the Revolutionary War, a state senator, and a member of the state convention that ratified the Constitution of the United States. Over the right fireplace is a portrait of Franklin's great-grandfather, James Roosevelt, who was a New York City merchant, a state assemblyman, an alderman, and the first of the family to settle in Dutchess County in 1819.

Ellen Emmett Rand painted the large portrait of Franklin D. Roosevelt at Hyde Park in 1932. It also hangs in the living room. The two highback leather chairs at the end of the room were Franklin Roosevelt's when he was governor of New York. He received a chair for each of his two-year terms. He always sat in the one on the left.

The Dresden Room on the main floor takes its name from the delicately wrought Dresden chandelier and mantel set that James Roosevelt purchased

The inviting living room at Hyde Park contains a Roosevelt portrait painted in 1932.

in Germany in 1866. The rug is an Aubusson. Sara Roosevelt chose the floral drapes and the matching upholstery in 1939, shortly before the king and queen of England visited here.

Quiet now, the dining room often buzzed with the dinner chatter of growing children and the conversation of distinguished guests. Just off the dining room is the Smoking Room where Roosevelt and his political associates tallied voting returns on many election nights.

Climbing the stairs to the second floor, one wonders how the paralyzed president ascended and descended. The house guide explains that a luggage trunk elevator connects the two floors. Upstairs you discover the Boyhood Bedroom, used by the young Franklin and his sons after him. The many notables who visited the Roosevelts were assigned rooms on the river side of the hall. Roosevelt was born in the master bedroom of the house prior to the 1915 expansion.

At the end of the hallway, in the new stone wing over the living room, is Roosevelt's bedroom, which contains his favorite naval prints and family photographs. Fala's leash and blanket are on the Scottie's own chair. Scat-

Viewing Franklin D. Roosevelt's bedroom at Hyde Park, the visitor's eye is drawn to the wheelchair he used after he was disabled by polio.

tered about the room are the books and magazines that were here at the time of Roosevelt's last visit in March 1945.

On January 15, 1944, President Roosevelt's home was designated a National Historic Site. A gift from the president, it consisted of thirty-three acres containing his house, its outbuildings, and his chosen gravesite in the family rose garden. Three days after the his death on April 15, 1945, he was buried there.

When Mrs. Roosevelt and her children waived their life interests in the house and the grounds, title to the area was accepted by the secretary of the interior. The site was formally dedicated on April 12, 1946, the first anniversary of the president's death. It now spans 290 acres. Mrs. Roosevelt was buried beside her husband on November 10, 1962.

Approximately two hours from New York City, the museum of the Franklin D. Roosevelt Library is open 9:00 A.M. to 5:00 P.M. daily except Thanksgiving, Christmas, and New Year's Day. One admission fee is charged for entrance to both the library-museum and the home, located at 511 Albany Post Road, Hyde Park, New York 12538. Telephone: (914) 229-8114.

The home is closed Tuesday and Wednesday, November through March. For information on the Roosevelt Home, telephone (914) 229-9115.

NOTES

1. William R. Emerson, "Remarks of President Roosevelt at the laying of the cornerstone of the Roosevelt Library, November 9, 1939," signed by him, in "Materials," Exhibit VIII.

2. Raymond Geselbracht, "The Four Eras in the History of Presidential Papers," *Prologue, Journal of the National Archives* 15, no. 1 (Spring 1983): 38.

3. National Park Service, U.S. Department of the Interior, *Home of Franklin D. Roosevelt,* pamphlet.

CHAPTER 4

Harry S. Truman

Following the unexpected death of President Franklin D. Roosevelt on April 12, 1945, Vice President Harry S. Truman, a Democrat, became the nation's thirty-third president. He had been vice president only eighty-three days. He completed Roosevelt's term and was elected to one of his own (1949–1953).

L IKE HIS PREDECESSOR in office, Roosevelt, President Truman's first thought was to locate his library on family property, a portion of farmland in Grandview, Missouri. That plan, however, was gladly laid aside when the town of Independence, where he lived before and after his presidency, offered to donate a park for that purpose. The site was (and is) a quiet and picturesque thirteen-acre knoll, more accessible than Grandview. Better yet, it is merely a mile from the Truman home at 219 Delaware. "All partisanship and selfishness were left behind months ago and this home city of this world-famous statesman is the most logical place to establish such a national shrine as the Harry S. Truman Library," reported the *Kansas City Times*.[1]

Seventeen thousand individuals and organizations contributed to the construction of the Truman Library. Designed by local architect Alonzo H. Gentry with the assistance of Edward Neild, the building was completed in two years. It is one story, long and low, crescent-shaped, and made of Indiana limestone. The style has been described as "modern," although the main entrance has square columns that give it a classic Egyptian look. With its full basement the building has 96,612 square feet of floor space.

Visitors entering the spacious lobby of the library building are immediately drawn toward the wall-sized, historic mural, "Independence and the Opening of the West," by Thomas Hart Benton. While you contemplate its message and vivid colors, a staff member might inform you that the former president was personally invited to climb the scaffolding to add a few brush strokes. Then it's time to proceed to the auditorium for a message from and about the library's namesake. A video presentation provides the information, but it is the voice and the presence of Harry S. Truman that captures your attention.

Citizen Truman often walked the mile from his home to the entrance of the Harry S. Truman Library where he had his office.

Truman was known for his six and one-half day work weeks at the library. One can almost see the former president striding the halls to explain "the layout" of "my library." He is said to have moved about briskly, pausing frequently to greet groups of visitors, especially students. Early in the morning, before the staff arrived, he would sometimes answer the phone, telling callers the hours of operation or, in reply to further questions, saying he knew the answers because "this is the old man himself."

Today a visitor stepping into Truman's White House Oval Office receives a recorded welcome from its occupant. A sense of order reigns here. His desk looks the way it did in 1945. Truman biographer David McCullough described it in this way:

Its surface, by FDR's standards, was bare and tidy. Besides a large green blotter and telephone, there were several pairs of eyeglasses in separate cases, two small metal ashtrays for visitors, a model cannon, a clock, two pen sets (one fancy, one plain), pencils, date stamp, calendar, two magnifying glasses, paste jar, glass inkwell, and a battered old ice-water vacuum pitcher, the one item from among FDR's personal effects that Truman has asked to keep.[2]

Later in his administration, Truman added to his desk the famous "The Buck Stops Here" sign.

On either side of the Oval Office mantel are paintings of George Washington and the great Latin American liberator, Simon Bolivar. Remington's painting titled "Fired On" claims the center spot. Its Indian fighters on horseback were said to remind Truman of deeds from his own days of military service. Before the fireplace is a world globe presented to President Truman by Gen. Dwight D. Eisenhower. In his recorded message the president points out two almost-hidden closed doors to the left and the right of the fireplace. It feels as though he is confiding in you, bringing you into his inner circle of those who once had special access to him.

Once a major renovation, launched on April 20, 1994, is completed, the Oval Office will become the focal point of a new "White House Gallery." The exhibit will review the official duties of the president and introduce President Truman's White House staff. The "Presidential Gallery," scheduled to open by the fall of 1996, will chronologically cover the domestic and international issues faced by President Truman—the end of World War II, McCarthyism and the Korean War, the 1948 presidential campaign, and the emerging Cold War. Another new exhibit that is being planned is titled "The Truman Legacy." It will show how many current developments and public policies had their roots in the Truman era.

Harry S. Truman became famous for the saying "The Buck Stops Here," which he displayed on his desk.

The museum in the library building will be open throughout the renovation.[3] Some items currently displayed may be moved, stored, or placed in temporary exhibits. Of particular interest are the table and chair Truman used to sign the Truman Doctrine, a foreign policy designed to contain communism, and the piano President Truman often played, which was donated to the White House by the Steinway Company in 1937 and given by President Richard M. Nixon to the Truman Library in 1969. In addition, there is a large exhibition of Truman family portraits by Greta Kempton, once described as the court painter of the Truman administration.[4]

Downstairs begins the "Harry S. Truman, Man from Missouri" time line. One of the first scripts explains the meaning behind the mysterious middle initial S. "When his first child was born on May 8, 1884, John Truman proudly nailed a muleshoe over his Lamar, Missouri, front door to celebrate the event. He and his wife named the boy Harry S., the "S" honoring both grandfathers: Anderson Shipp Truman and Solomon Young."[5]

Writings and photographs help chronicle Truman's childhood; his courtship and marriage to Elizabeth Virginia Wallace (his "Bess") on June 28, 1919; the birth of their only child, Margaret, on February 17, 1924; his management of a men's clothing store; his career as a judge in Jackson County, Missouri (1922–1924, 1926–1934); and his life-long interest in music and history. "I was beginning to realize—40 years before I had any thought of becoming president of the United States—that almost all current events in the affairs of government and nations have their parallels and precedents in the past," he said.

Truman was strongly influenced by his experience as a soldier in France during World War I. Visitors see the khaki combat uniform and equipment of Captain Harry S. Truman. Nearby weapons include a 75 millimeter field artillery gun and caisson Model 1918 that inspired the "Artillery Song" popular during World War I. Its lyrics, "and the caissons go rolling along," have become part of American history.

Truman is said to have proclaimed his tenure as the senator for Missouri as the happiest ten years of his life (1935–1945). When President Roosevelt, running for his fourth term, asked Senator Truman to join the ticket, he was not eager to accept. One photo shows him at the 1944 Democratic Convention with his hand extended, palm forward, resisting the vice-presidential nomination. Then you read FDR's deciding words: "Well, you can tell him, if he wants to break up the Democratic party in the middle of a war, that's his responsibility!"

A reluctant vice president, Truman soon had the presidency thrust upon him. This black headline from the *Kansas City Times* tells all: "Roosevelt Dies; Truman Goes In." Truman admitted that he felt as if "the moon, the

Pictured on the Capitol steps, Truman was elected to the U.S. Senate in 1934 where he supported Roosevelt's New Deal legislation.

stars and all the planets had just fallen on me." He was sworn in at 7:09 P.M. on April 12, 1945, and immediately replaced Roosevelt at Yalta in the Soviet Union. Truman photographs, handwritten notes, and letters help explain the chartering of the United Nations and the decision to drop the atomic bomb on Japan to end the war. With peace came more challenges: Palestine, the

Iron Curtain, and the Potsdam Conference. Truman's words justify the Marshall Plan: "Foreign policy has been costly, but World War III would be ten times as costly."

Truman's Point Four Inaugural Address of 1949 focused on America's citizens and the government's desire to produce more food, more clothing, more materials for housing, and more mechanical power to lighten their burdens. Yet it is obvious that the president's burdens remained heavy. Concerned with defense, displays cover the hydrogen bomb, NATO, the communist threat, and the Korean conflict, including the president's controversial decision to fire Gen. Douglas MacArthur. And along with everything else,

Pat Nixon, and Harry and Bess Truman form an appreciative audience as President Richard Nixon plays a tune on a White House piano donated to the Truman Library.

President Harry S. Truman pinned a medal on General Douglas MacArthur at their October 15, 1950, meeting on Wake Island. Truman called the meeting to discuss MacArthur's strategy in Korea but fired him six months later for insubordination.

the White House required heavy renovation. A copy of the *Report of the Commission on the Renovation of the Executive Mansion* is on display. Its contents convinced Truman that the building was "standing up purely by habit." Truman had it "reduced to a shell and rebuilt with a steel frame." A genuine "White House Table," crafted from materials removed during the 1949–1952 reconstruction of the White House, uniquely records this feat. Given to President Truman by the Radio Correspondents' Association, it includes pine wood from President Lincoln's original 1817 bedroom floor, maple wood from President Truman's bedroom, nails taken from the second floor, and other tokens from the first floor.

Also on display downstairs is a section of Truman's "Farewell Address to the American People," delivered in 1953. "The President—whoever he is—has to decide," he said in that speech. "He can't pass the buck to anybody. No one else can do the deciding for him. That's his job." Pausing, your eyes drift to an oil portrait of a solemn Truman with the U.S. Capitol in the background.

Lighter moments are captured in the Museum as well. A map shows the miles covered during Truman's whistle stop campaign of 1948. Also displayed are items he received along the way: boxing gloves, keys to various cities, and special honors such as the "Order of the Golden Plow" from the city of Des Moines, Iowa. A four-color cutout shows a beaming Truman holding up the now-famous yet erroneous *Chicago Daily Tribune* headline: "Dewey Defeats Truman." Equally telling is the *Saturday Evening Post* magazine cover by Norman Rockwell. Titled "Family Squabble," it shows a young couple at breakfast. Each has a newspaper, his the *Tribune* supporting Dewey, hers the *Reformer* supporting Truman. Then there is the "I'm Just Wild About Harry" sheet music with words and music by Noble Sissle and Eubie Blake.

Various cars driven by the Trumans are parked in the gallery. One of the more interesting is from the White House fleet, a 1950 twenty-foot Lincoln Cosmopolitan Limousine with a V-8 engine. It has two heaters front and back, four cigarette lighters, two collapsible seats, and a hydraulically operated window system. The red, white, and blue license plate reads "Inaugural 1" with the "District of Columbia" beneath it. The Capitol and a shield of stars and stripes complete it.

Before leaving, there is time to pause at the gravesites of President and

Although almost everyone predicted his defeat, Harry S. Truman ran against New York's Governor Thomas Dewey in 1948 and won his bid for the presidency.

Mrs. Truman in the library courtyard. The flat stone covering his grave has the presidential seal at its head and lists the many positions he held during his long lifetime: judge, presiding judge, U.S. senator from Missouri, vice president, president. The U.S. Senate and the Jackson County, Missouri, seals are also shown. Bess Wallace Truman's stone has a wreath and flowers at its head. Her life is summed up simply: Married Harry S. Truman, daughter Margaret, First Lady.

From the courtyard you can look in on the office in the library that Truman used from 1957 to 1966. Here he was visited by important dignitaries that included former presidents Hoover, Eisenhower, Kennedy, and Johnson. His desk, which once stood in his White House study, looks as though he just left it. Books from his extensive, personal collection line the walls, and there is an impressive collection of family photos. Through another court-yard window, you can also view a portion of the library's research section.

Outside on the library grounds you'll find a Bicentennial Time Capsule that celebrates Truman's interest in history. Containing materials from 1776 to 1976, it is due to be opened May 8, 2076. Close by is a reproduction of the Liberty Bell from Independence Hall in Philadelphia. Given to the City of Independence by the city of Annecy-le-Vieux in France, it is appropriately "Dedicated to you, A free Citizen in a free land."

Ten miles east of downtown Kansas City, Missouri, the museum of the Truman Library is open 9:00 A.M. to 5:00 P.M. daily except Thanksgiving, Christmas, and New Year's Day. An admission fee is charged for visitors over fifteen years of age except students in organized tour groups for whom application has been made in advance. The library is located at U.S. Highway 24 and Delaware, Independence, Missouri 64050. Telephone: (816) 833-1225 for recorded message and special events or (816) 833-1400.

Tours of the nearby Truman Home, 219 Delaware Street, are operated by the National Park Service. The home is open daily 9:00 A.M. to 5:00 P.M. from Memorial Day through Labor Day. Closed Mondays, Labor Day, and Memorial Day. An admission fee is charged for adults (ages seventeen to sixty-two). Eight people can tour the home every fifteen minutes. Telephone: (816) 254-9929.

NOTES

1. David McCullough, *Truman* (New York: Simon & Schuster, 1992), 943.
2. McCullough, *Truman*, 403.
3. Harry S. Truman Library, "Museum Renovation Plans To Be Unveiled at Truman Library," news release, April 20, 1994.
4. This information was provided by the staff of the Harry S. Truman Library.
5. This quotation and the other Truman quotations in this chapter are from written or recorded scripts in the Harry S. Truman Library. For general information about the museum, see the pamphlet titled *Harry S. Truman Library and Museum* published by the Harry S. Truman Library, National Archives and Records Administration.

CHAPTER 5

Dwight D. Eisenhower

LIBRARY DEDICATED: MAY 1, 1962

ABILENE, KANSAS

Dwight D. Eisenhower, a Republican, was sworn into office on
January 20, 1953, and served two terms as president (1953–1957, 1957–1961).

ARRIVING AT THE Eisenhower Center in the rural town of Abilene, you discover a complex of five buildings: the library, the Visitors Center, the family home (on its original site), the museum, and the Place of Meditation. The setting is that of a college campus where one is free to stroll about, enjoying several park-like acres of flat, pleasant grounds. It is watched over by an eleven-foot statue of Eisenhower, the soldier.

Here is the first sign that this presidential library will differ significantly from those dedicated to career politicians. Dwight D. Eisenhower, a five-star general, had already achieved his lifetime goal as a highly decorated military leader before answering the call to serve as president of the United States.

This is a message you will hear again as you view the orientation film on Eisenhower's life and work in the Visitors Center auditorium. But a second theme is also heard. Although he was a soldier, Eisenhower always sought peace. He stated this clearly during the library's ground breaking on October 13, 1959:

When this library is filled with documents, and scholars come here to probe into some of the facts of the past half century, I hope that they, as we today, are concerned primarily with the ideas, principles, and trends that provide guides to a free, rich peaceful future in which all peoples can achieve ever-rising levels of human well-being.[1]

The Family Home

Before entering the museum, visitors generally tour the home occupied by Eisenhower family members from 1898 through 1946, the year Ida Elizabeth Stover Eisenhower, the president's mother, died. Soon after, her sons gave the house, a two-story cottage typical of Kansas homes in the late nine-

This eleven-foot statue of Eisenhower, the soldier, was a gift from former Kansas senator Harry Darby. Dedicated on June 15, 1985, it rests on a five-sided pedestal of Georgia granite.

teenth century, to the Eisenhower Foundation. Inside, family furniture and mementos remain arranged as they were then.

Trained guides point out that the front parlor was off-limits to the Eisenhower brood of six boys, but life in the back parlor was far from dull. It holds the newest of radios for that time, one with a short wave band. You see a worn, wooden rocker boasting a pillow bearing all of the boys' names. Nearby is a 110-year-old piano, which their mother played well. All her sons took lessons on it. The family photographs lining the walls tell the story of a large, robust family that thrived on traditional values.

The house grew over the years. A bathroom was added when Dwight D., nicknamed "Ike," was eighteen. The kitchen was added when he graduated

The Eisenhower family home is a simple frame structure, typical of Kansas in the late nineteenth century.

from West Point. One item of special interest is a dough box that Ida Eisenhower used to bake nine loaves of bread every two days.

The Museum

With its clean, modern lines constructed of Kansas limestone, the museum building designed by Wilton Beckett of Los Angeles stands in sharp contrast to the Victorian family home. Directly inside the front door are five mural panels painted by Louis Bouche and Ross Moffett. They depict Eisenhower's life and career from early childhood through his service as America's thirty-fourth president. Embedded in the floor before the panels is a symbol that will be seen again within the museum's Military Gallery, a sword standing on its hilt with flames shooting from it. It is the emblem of the Supreme Headquarters Allied Expeditionary Force (SHAEF), which Eisenhower commanded.

Entering the rooms with the collections is like stepping into someone's attic. The five major galleries are arranged chronologically (Introductory, Temporary, First Lady's, Military, and Presidential) and are filled with mementos of all kinds and sizes.

The Introductory Gallery is a natural starting place. Having already toured the Family Home, visitors look with interest at the 1902 family portrait of David and Ida Eisenhower with their six surviving sons. (A seventh child died.) Ike's interest in high school athletics, particularly baseball and football, and his education at West Point, beginning in 1911 at the age of twenty, are explained in this gallery. Eisenhower's West Point class, the "class the stars fell on," produced a record number of generals. A script explains: "More than one-third of its 164 members earned at least one star by the end of their careers. Two of them, Dwight D. Eisenhower and Omar N. Bradley, achieved the highest rank possible in the U.S. Army—General of the Army."

West Point gave Eisenhower a free college education and an opportunity to play football again. After he was sidelined by a knee injury, he turned to coaching fellow cadets. One especially interesting display contains his school uniforms.

Graduation from West Point resulted in a first assignment at Fort Sam Houston, Texas, where he met Mamie Geneva Doud, who was visiting the area. Photographs and memorabilia chronicle their meeting, engagement on Valentine's Day 1916, and marriage on July 1, 1916. Numerous army postings followed. Their first son, Doud Dwight, was born on September 18, 1917. Unfortunately, he died of scarlet fever in 1921. It was a sorrow Eisenhower was said to carry all of his life.

Shown on their wedding day, Second Lieutenant Eisenhower and Mamie Geneva Doud were married on July 1, 1916.

Complementing this personal record is a collection of World War I posters and an exhibit that emphasizes Eisenhower's love of history. During the years 1930 to 1935, he was stationed in Washington, D.C., to work on the American Battle Monuments Commission (ABMC) under another highly recognizable figure, Gen. John J. Pershing.

Various activities during the late nineteen-twenties, thirties, and early forties are presented via weathered maps, photographs, and a diary/journal. One begun in 1929, the Eisenhower/Gruber Diary, documents a seventeen-day, 1,800-mile motor trip through four Western European countries. "Paris Aug. 28. Harrowing climb over the Feuka Pass in Switzerland Sept. 5; final segment completed by Gruber [a military associate and friend] May 1940."

Objects in this area recall a variety of events from the Eisenhower years. There is an intricate, miniature bamboo house Ike brought back for Mamie's mother from the Philippines, where he was stationed from 1935 to 1939.

On June 6, 1944, D-Day, General Eisenhower gave the order to launch the Allied invasion of Normandy. The D-Day planning table, a mahogany Sheraton pedestal table with twelve Chippendale chairs, is protected in the gallery by a see-through plastic barrier. A silver plaque reads:

This table was in constant use Oct. 1943 to May 1944 for the deliberations of Gen. Eisenhower Allied Commander-in-Chief and his staff who were then planning the Victorious Allied Advance in Germany. It was also used by Gen. Marshall and Joint Chiefs of Staff of the United States Army when plans for "D" Day were put into operation whilst staying at Stanwell House, England, May to June 1944.

Visitors also can see a photo time line that begins in 1890 with Eisenhower's birth in Denison, Texas, and ends in 1969 with his funeral.

Alaska and Hawaii became states during Eisenhower's presidency. Public Law 86-3, which made Hawaii a state, is displayed. Another exhibit shows Eisenhower as the "Traveling President." Included are photographs and models of *Barbara Anne,* the presidential yacht; *Columbine III,* the presidential plane, a Super Constellation; and the first presidential helicopter, a Bell H-13J (USAF).

Visitors learn that presidential gifts reached new heights during the Eisenhower years, both in number and originality. Visitors see a Bing & Grondahl porcelain elephant from Copenhagen, Denmark; a silver vase given in 1955 by His Holiness Athesagora, patriarch of Constantinople, Turkey; and a silver tea service, the gift of Dr. Sukarno, president of the Republic of Indonesia, in 1956.

Mamie Eisenhower's history is documented in the First Lady's Gallery through photographs and scripts. You learn that she was from a well-to-do family. One of the first items pictured is a 1914 Rauch & Lang electric automobile that belonged to her parents, Mr. and Mrs. John S. Doud. Ike occasionally drove this, a luxury car in its day. Cost: $4,300.

More personal details about the First Lady are noted as well. Mamie loved high fashion design and was a trend setter. She made the list of the "Ten Best Dressed Women" every year she was First Lady. Her hairstyle, which swept the country, was called the "Mamie-look." There is even a cover letter and diagram from Elizabeth Arden showing how it is set. And if anyone wonders what Mamie's goal in life was, there are these words: "Ike was my career. I never pretended to be anything but Ike's wife." Quite fittingly, there is the family lineage. Son: Doud Dwight (deceased). Son: John Sheldon Doud married Barbara Thompson 1947. Grandchildren: Dwight David II, Barbara Anne, Susan, and Mary Jean.

Mamie's White House duties centered on supervising the staff and hospitality. The Eisenhowers received 102 official and unofficial visits from heads of state and heads of government during their eight years in the White House. Clothing, jewelry, and hats worn by Mrs. Eisenhower are shown.

Visitors see a formal fiftieth wedding anniversary portrait with the nota-

General Dwight D. Eisenhower respected and revered his soldiers. They recognized and re-turned his trust.

tion July 1, 1916–1966. A neighboring exhibit chronicles Mamie Doud Eisen-hower moving from girlhood to marriage. It contains both her wedding dress and a reproduction of her wedding cake.

An active volunteer, Mrs. Eisenhower raised funds for medical research and numerous humanitarian projects, activities that she continued after her husband's death. She was also interested in arts and cultural events. A sym-bol of the high regard in which she was held is a shimmering replica of the vessel the USS *Constitution*. It was created by artist Mitsugi Ohno and pre-sented to her in 1971.

The Military Gallery begins with Eisenhower's role as the Supreme Com-mander during the European conflict, and the men and women who served under him. The SHAEF emblem, a sword standing on its hilt with flames

The Order of Bath, the highest honor bestowed on a foreign citizen for distinguished service, was given to Dwight D. Eisenhower by the British government. It is part of the museum's permanent D-Day exhibit.

shooting from it, is seen. You are surrounded by the tools of war: guns, battle dress uniforms, weapons used during World War II, war plans on paper, and medals awarded and received. Dated news film is shown. Model ships, an armored utility car (the M-20), and a quarter ton, 4 by 4 jeep, restored to World War II standards, add to the story.

There is also a 1942 Cadillac Staff Car retired in 1956, the speedometer registering nearly 200,000 miles. Its history is complex. The car was assigned to Eisenhower during World War II. Following his army retirement, he used it in New York when he was president of Columbia University, then in Europe when he was appointed by President Truman as Supreme Commander of the North Atlantic Treaty Organization (NATO). In 1955 the car was sent to Geneva for President Eisenhower's use at a summit conference. It was bought in 1956, restored, and brought to the Museum for permanent display.

The Presidential Gallery shows Eisenhower in his role as president through campaign pieces, photos, and other memorabilia. The "Eisenhower Crystal," made of Steuben glass, celebrates his crusade for peace in the world. This stunning creation designed by Donald Pollard features an eagle with scales weighing the two halves of the world globe. It is monogrammed "DDE," with the dates 1953–1961. Multisided, its message reads: "Peace and Friendship in Freedom with Justice for All Mankind." Eisenhower commonly gave and received Steuben crystal as gifts during his presidency.

A Bible given to the president by his mother upon his graduation from West Point is exhibited. The Presidential Gallery also includes a bronze medal commemorating Inauguration Day 1953 and the Presidential Prayer. A black and white photograph shows him at the desk he used to write it. The desk itself is displayed, with his glasses and writing paper lying on top.

You turn a corner and find a painting from the president's Oval Office. Underneath, mounted on wooden door-sized planks, are these words from Eisenhower's book *Mandate for Change:*

On January 21, 1953, shortly after 7:30 A.M. I entered the oval room of the West Wing of the White House, destined to be my office for the next eight years. The office of President of the United States as compared to the sumptuous quarters of many business leaders and of most Cabinet officials, is a surprisingly plain room. I had been in it many times before; its simplicity seemed to be most appropriate for the American head of state.

Following this introduction are photographs of the Oval Office and other rooms in the White House. There are objects from Eisenhower's Oval Office as well: an oil painting by Olaf Wieghorst, "Apache Scouts"; bronze sculp-

Dwight D. Eisenhower was the first president to hold a televised news conference. His press secretary, however, edited it before it was shown to the public.

tures by Charles M. Russell, "The Medicine Man" and "The Robe Flesher"; and a bronze by Frederic Remington, "Broncho Buster." The president's interest in the Old West is surely demonstrated here.

Moving on, you come to photos of the cabinet and the White House staff, doodles made by Eisenhower on agendas for cabinet meetings (a bicycle, a sled, a tree, and more), plus an explanation of the White House reorganization in 1954 when Eisenhower added more personal staff and a press secretary. Dated movie film shows a press conference, and there is a walnut podium used by Eisenhower during various appearances between 1953 and 1960.

An especially interesting display features the president's brother, Milton Eisenhower, who served presidents before and after the Eisenhower terms.

Mention is made of Presidents Coolidge, Hoover, Roosevelt, and Truman, who preceded Eisenhower, and Presidents Kennedy, Johnson, and Nixon, who followed.

There is a photo arcade of the departments functioning during the Eisenhower years—Defense; State; Labor; Health, Education and Welfare; and Interior—plus a listing of three of his memoirs: *Mandate for Change, Waging Peace,* and *At Ease.*

After serving two terms as president, Eisenhower moved to Gettysburg, Pennsylvania, where he had a retirement office at Gettysburg College from 1961 to 1968. Re-created in the museum, his office contains, in addition to the usual furnishings, a golf club, an elephant standing on its trunk (a gift from a trucking company), photos of his four grandchildren, and numerous Steuben glass collectibles. The Eisenhowers' home was located just four miles from this office.

Exiting the museum and continuing around the perimeter of the complex, you come to five embossed metal panels forming a memorial wall, placed there by the Kansas Society of the Daughters of the American Revolution. One panel reads: "From the modest home built on these acres came one destined to lead in battle the mightiest array of fighting forces ever to wage war in freedom's cause. The victory secure, as president he led the effort to ensure a continuing peace for all the world."

The Eisenhower statue in the center of these grounds is fittingly titled "Champion of Peace." A gift to the people of the United States from Harry Darby, a former U.S. senator from Kansas, it was dedicated on June 15, 1985. The pedestal upon which it stands carries these accomplishments: "General, Supreme Commander, Chief of Staff, U.S. Army, Supreme Allied Commander, and President U.S."

The Eisenhower Library has an exterior of Kansas limestone in sharp contrast to the interior's extensive use of marble.

The Library

The library occupies a separate building directly across from the museum. Only a small portion is open to the public. But it is particularly noteworthy that President Eisenhower signed the Presidential Library Act of 1955 that firmly established the Presidential Library System.

Place of Meditation

One last building remains to be visited, the Place of Meditation. Outside stands a fountain, and carillon bells may be pealing "America the Beautiful." Inside is the final resting place of this accomplished man. Water softly flows down a golden wall carved with these words from "The Chance for Peace," an address delivered by President Eisenhower in Washington, D.C., on April

The Place of Meditation is the final resting place of Dwight D. Eisenhower, Mamie Doud Eisenhower, and their firstborn son, Doud Dwight Eisenhower.

16, 1953: "Every gun made, every warship launched, every rocket fired signifies, in the final sense, a theft from those who are cold and are not clothed . . . This is not a way of life at all . . . Under the cloud of threatening war, it is humanity hanging from a cross of iron."

Before the wall lie the graves of Dwight David Eisenhower and Mamie Doud Eisenhower. Between them is the grave of their son Doud Dwight (1917–1921). The chapel was designed by architect John Brink.

Located in Abilene, Kansas, the Eisenhower Center is two miles south of the Abilene exit, off Interstate 70 on Kansas Highway 15 (also called Buckeye Avenue). All buildings at the Center are open every day, from 9:00 A.M. to 4:45 P.M. throughout the year with the exception of Thanksgiving, Christmas, and New Year's Day. During the summer, beginning on Memorial Day, the museum and Visitors Center are open until 5:45 P.M.

A small fee is charged for admission to the exhibit areas of the museum. Children under sixteen are admitted free. No fee is charged at the other buildings.

For additional information, telephone (913) 263-4751.

NOTE

1. "Dwight D. Eisenhower Library," pamphlet published by the National Archives and Records Administration.

CHAPTER 6

John Fitzgerald Kennedy

Elected to his first term as president (1961–1965), John Fitzgerald Kennedy,

a Democrat, was sworn into office on January 20, 1961. He died

from an assassin's bullet less than three years later on November 22, 1963.

WHEN THE John Fitzgerald Kennedy Library was dedicated on October 20, 1979, its museum contained exhibits that, to be fully appreciated, depended on personal memories of John and Robert Kennedy and of the Kennedy administration. Later surveys by the museum staff indicated, however, that half of the visitors were under age forty and lacked this basic foundation. Therefore, a complete renovation was planned. The new presentation was designed to introduce the life, leadership, and legacy of President Kennedy; to convey his enthusiasm for politics; and to illustrate the nature of the office of president for these younger generations.

When the "new" museum completed its $6.9 million project and was opened on October 29, 1993, President Bill Clinton delivered the dedication address. "The 21st century can be our century," he said, "if we approach it with the vigor, the determination, the wisdom and the sheer confidence and joy of life that John Kennedy brought to America in 1960."[1] Clinton also recalled a visit he made to the White House in 1963 with other participants in the Boy's Nation leadership program. Clinton said he felt called to public service after shaking hands with President Kennedy in the Rose Garden.

At the dedication Sen. Edward Kennedy, the president's younger brother, echoed Clinton's theme of public service: "It is our hope that the Museum will be a source of education and inspiration to the Greater Boston community and to visitors throughout the world and will encourage those who come here to dedicate themselves to public service in their own communities."[2]

Columbia Point, overlooking Boston's harbor and skyline, is the perfect setting for designer I. M. Pei's dramatic 135,000 square foot building with a nine-story white, precast tower and glass-enclosed pavilion. The water, the new John T. Fallon State Pier, and the library's 9.5 acre park—landscaped

The John F. Kennedy Library is visited annually by approximately 200,000 visitors and schoolchildren who tour the museum, 2,000 researchers who work in the research rooms, and 40,000 people who participate in community events and educational programs.

with pine trees, shrubs, and wild roses—give the visitor a sense of Kennedy's beloved Cape Cod. The president's sloop *Victura,* cradled on the lawn and oriented toward Boston Harbor, completes the waterfront scene.

Inside Pei's impressive structure, visitors are introduced to President Kennedy in a lively and personal way. He speaks out in his own words throughout the Museum in three theaters and twenty video presentations. The first encounter occurs during a seventeen-minute introductory film made by Academy Award-winning director Peter Davis. President Kennedy engagingly describes highlights (originally captured in a 1952 television interview) from his childhood and education, his wartime service in the South Pacific, and his early political career. You learn that he was born in Brookline, Massachusetts, on May 29, 1917, the second son of financier Joseph P. Kennedy and Rose Fitzgerald Kennedy; he graduated from Harvard in 1940; he rescued several of his crewmen when the boat he was commanding, PT-109, was rammed by a Japanese destroyer off the Solomon Islands; he was elected by Massachusetts voters to serve in the U.S. House of Representatives in 1946; and he was elected to the U.S. Senate in 1952.

Leaving the theater, you are transported in time back to the early 1960s. The exhibit begins with the Los Angeles Convention Hall where "JFK" wins the Democratic presidential nomination in 1960. The feeling of being alive in the 1960s is enhanced by a re-creation of Main Street in Anytown, USA. Glancing into the windows of an appliance store, you see a television broadcasting 1960 programs and commercials. One prime-time show is "Father Knows Best."

Then the real work of the 1960 campaign begins. Moving on, you accompany Sen. John F. Kennedy and his opponent, Vice President Richard M. Nixon, on the presidential campaign trail. A video shows them kissing babies and shaking hands with voters, while offering two different visions for America. A storefront headquarters for the Kennedy campaign is filled with memorabilia. Photographs, itineraries, maps, and memos document the involvement of the entire Kennedy clan, particularly his brother and campaign manager Robert F. Kennedy, in JFK's bid for the presidency.

As this campaign neared its climax, four Kennedy-Nixon debates were held. Visitors can watch Senator Kennedy, clearly at ease before the camera, verbally jousting with his Republican opponent in the Chicago studio where the first televised presidential debate occurred. Then it's on to election night

Delivering a sense of time and place, this museum display evokes the sights and sounds of the 1960 Democratic National Convention in Los Angeles.

Museum visitors watch the two candidates, Kennedy and Nixon, debate the political issues in a stylized setting. The display includes the original soundboard of the Chicago television studio where the first presidential debate occurred.

Known for his charm and charisma, John F. Kennedy campaigns for the presidency in West Virginia in 1960.

with Walter Cronkite and CBS News reporting on the returns of this close contest.

Next, seated in an open theater, you "attend" the inauguration and see John F. Kennedy, the youngest president and the first Roman Catholic ever elected, deliver his memorable inaugural address. "Ask not what your country can do for you; ask what you can do for your country," he challenges his listeners. Lending atmosphere to the scene are a newsstand of periodicals and a souvenir stand exhibiting memorabilia created for the occasion.

Stroll through a portal and you enter a different environment, that of "The Presidency." A long, colonnaded corridor with a marble floor, red carpeting, and woodwork takes you into the White House. Connecting corridors lead to exhibits on the Kennedy presidency.

You meet members of the Kennedy administration and then proceed into rooms addressing the issues they faced. The room on international affairs introduces a wide array of topics. They include President Kennedy's meeting in Vienna with Soviet premier Nikita Khrushchev; the confrontation over access to West Berlin; the aftermath of colonialism in southeast Asia that led to the deployment of 17,000 U.S. military advisors in South Vietnam; the failed U.S. invasion at the Bay of Pigs in Cuba; and the threat to the U.S. mainland from Soviet missiles in Cuba. The tension these topics created is real as Kennedy answers questions from the press during live television news conferences.

There is an inspiring and upbeat exhibit on the Peace Corps, created by executive order in 1961 to send volunteers to other countries. Originally an agency of the Department of State, it is now an independent agency of the U.S. government. Training materials, a journal kept by a volunteer, and gifts sent from host countries are on display. Visitors can view early Peace Corps recruiting films and get caught up in the spirit of its earliest days.

A twenty-minute documentary portrays the president, government leaders, diplomats, news commentators, and ordinary citizens at the time of the Soviet missile crisis in October 1962. The film chronicles the installation of the missiles in Cuba; the bold naval blockade by the United States to prevent the arrival of more; the tense negotiations with the Soviet Union when the world held its breath; and the final resolution of the crisis. The film attempts to present all points of view objectively so visitors can judge history on their own terms.

Film is also used to illustrate President Kennedy's commitment to the manned space program. Viewers become caught up in the countdown and the launch of Alan Shepard's spacecraft on May 5, 1961, the day he became the first American in space. The film also shows astronauts in training and receiving awards at the White House, and the exciting visits by President Kennedy to Cape Canaveral, Florida, in 1962. Significant artifacts include memos from the president to National Air and Space Administration personnel, models of early manned spacecraft, and a replica of the space suit of John Glenn, the first man to orbit the Earth.

Arms control was another important issue for this president. In a room reminiscent of the White House Treaty Room, visitors can see a copy of the Limited Nuclear Test Ban Treaty with the Soviet Union and Great Britain and watch excerpts from two of President Kennedy's speeches on peace and disarmament. Addressing the graduating class at American University on June 10, 1963, President Kennedy said: "Today the expenditure of billions of dollars every year on weapons acquired for the purpose of making sure we never need to use them is essential to keeping the peace. But surely the acquisition of such idle stockpiles—which can only destroy and never create—is not the only, much less the most efficient, means of assuring peace."[3]

A re-creation of the Justice Department office of Robert F. Kennedy, when

In 1962 John Glenn became the first American to orbit the earth. He holds an American flag with John F. Kennedy.

he was attorney general, follows. Initiatives and programs he was involved with include civil rights, organized crime, poverty law, and youth crime. He also had a unique role in advising and representing his brother in a wide variety of matters, especially international diplomacy.

Next you enter the Oval Office as it appeared on June 11, 1963. A speech is being made, President Kennedy's address to the nation on civil rights. In a dramatic seven-minute video the speech is interspersed with clips of nonviolent demonstrators being dragged off by the police as the crowd sings "We Shall Overcome." In contrast, the furnishings in this room seem relatively unimportant: a replica of President Kennedy's desk, his rocking chair, and a globe of the world in 1961.

The museum's re-created Oval Office, as it looked during President Kennedy's televised address to the nation on civil rights on June 11, 1963, is the setting for a dramatic seven-minute video presentation.

In addition to being president, Kennedy was a family man. In 1953, while he was a U.S. senator, he married Jacqueline Bouvier. Her role as First Lady was far-reaching. She worked to advance the appreciation of the arts and encouraged preservation of America's heritage, especially the White House, which she refurbished. In 1962 she received an Emmy Award for her tour of the White House televised on CBS. Parts of the film are shown here. Visitors also can view models of the National Cultural Center she helped to develop. The National Cultural Center became the John F. Kennedy Center for the Performing Arts, a "living" memorial to the slain president by an act of Congress in 1964.

Jacqueline Kennedy's aristocratic background brought culture and the arts to the White House. The audience applauds while the cellist Pablo Casals takes a bow.

In a room suggesting the residential quarters of the White House, family photographs and mementos trace three generations of the president's family from their roots in Ireland. Scanning them, you recognize the commitment of public service handed down from generation to generation of the Kennedy family. Photographic and video images portray the president in quiet moments with his wife and children—Caroline Bouvier, born in 1957, and John F., Jr., born in 1960.

Leaving the splendor of the White House, viewers walk through a dark corridor. Four video screens show news clips from November 22, 1963. President Kennedy has been critically wounded by a sniper's bullet while riding in

Risking charges of nepotism, President John F. Kennedy named his brother Robert attorney general. Robert Kennedy's closeness and unquestionable loyalty to his brother allowed him to make suggestions and criticisms that no one else could.

an open limousine in Dallas, Texas. Walter Cronkite reports President Kennedy's death, and displays show how the nation and the world mourn his passing. Then the corridor widens into a circular space. This Reflection Room is lit only by nine illuminated, color transparencies of places around the world named after John F. Kennedy.

The museum concludes with the "Legacy" gallery, where visitors may explore archival documents and use interactive computers to discover insights into Kennedy initiatives and how those programs affect the world today. Social action programs begun and headed by Kennedy family members are also presented here, including the Special Olympics and Very Special Arts for the developmentally challenged.[4]

One corner is claimed by a 3.5 ton paint-spattered piece of the Berlin Wall donated by the German government. It is symbolic of the peaceful ending to the Cold War between the Soviet Union and the West and brings to mind President Kennedy's famous words when he visited Berlin on June 26, 1963: "Ich bin ein Berliner."

Tours end in a glass pavilion where an American flag, measuring forty-five by twenty-six feet, hangs suspended from the ceiling. And there is one last Kennedy quotation, his final call for public service: "All this will not be finished in the first one hundred days. Nor will it be finished in the first one thousand days, nor in the life of this administration, nor even perhaps in our lifetime on this planet. But let us begin."[5]

Accessible by car from I-93 to exit 14 (northbound) or exit 15 (southbound) and by boat, the John Fitzgerald Kennedy Library is open daily except Thanksgiving, Christmas, and New Year's Day. Hours are 9 A.M. to 5 P.M. Admission is charged except for children under six. The library is located at Columbia Point, Boston, Massachusetts 02125. Telephone: (617) 929-4523.

NOTES

1. John F. Kennedy Library Foundation, "The John F. Kennedy Library Newsletter," Winter 1993, 2. See also John Fitzgerald Kennedy Library, "President Clinton, Kennedy Family Dedicate New Museum at Kennedy Library," press release, December 6, 1993.

2. "Kennedy Library Newsletter," 3. See also Patti Hartigan, "JFK for a New Generation," *Boston Globe,* Living Arts, October 19, 1993, 61, 65.

3. Quoted in Theodore Sorensen, *Let the Word Go Forth* (New York: Dell, 1988).

4. For more information, see two fact sheets given out by the Library. They are titled "The John F. Kennedy Library" and "The New Museum at the John F. Kennedy Library."

5. Written script, John F. Kennedy Library.

CHAPTER 7

Lyndon Baines Johnson

—=«(»=—

LIBRARY DEDICATED: MAY 22, 1971
AUSTIN, TEXAS

Vice President Lyndon Baines Johnson, a Democrat, was sworn into office

on November 22, 1963, following the assassination of President Kennedy.

He completed the remainder of Kennedy's term (1963–1965) and was elected

to serve his own term (1965–1969).

THE MOST-VISITED of all of the presidential libraries and the first to be placed on a college campus, the Lyndon Baines Johnson Library is located at the University of Texas at Austin. With its accessible and urban campus, the university won out over other competitors for the Johnson Library when it proposed not only donating the property upon which it stands, but also establishing a graduate school of public affairs in conjunction with it. Although the Library itself remains the possession of the university, the National Archives is responsible for its administration.

A modern building on a thirty-acre site, the Library is monolithic in design and unrelieved by ornaments. Its eight stories of travertine marble stand on a knoll overlooking the campus. A wide plaza connects the building with the Lyndon Baines Johnson School of Public Affairs in Sid Richardson Hall.

Of the contemporary Library and the man he designed it for, architect Gordon Bunshaft has said: "I thought the president was a really virile man, a strong man with nothing sweet or sentimental or small about him. . . . I think this building is kind of powerful, and he's kind of a powerful guy."[1]

At the dedication of the Library on May 22, 1971, former president Johnson assessed the library's contents in this way:

It is all here; the story of our time—with the bark off. There is no record of a mistake, nothing critical, ugly or unpleasant that is not included in the files here. We have papers from my forty years in public service in one place for friend and foe to judge, to approve or disapprove. . . . This library will show the facts, not just the joy and triumphs, but the sorrow and failures, too.[2]

Entering the first floor exhibition hall, one encounters more travertine marble and an Orientation Theater that periodically shows a documentary

Like the man himself, the Lyndon Baines Johnson Library has a strong and towering presence.

film on Lyndon Johnson's life and career. On display are bronze busts of the president and Mrs. Johnson by sculptor Robert Berks. One exhibit, titled "First Family Tributes to Lady Bird Johnson," contains letters about her by White House residents ranging from Jackie Kennedy to Bill Clinton. Also on exhibit is a bronze bust of Dr. Martin Luther King by Robert Berks and an inscription of these words by President Johnson, spoken when the Library was dedicated: "I hope that visitors who come here will achieve a closer understanding of the ... Presidency ... and that the young people who come here will get a clearer comprehension of what this Nation tried to do in an eventful period of its history."

Like the Harry S. Truman Library, the Johnson Library is being renovated while the doors remain open. The redesign of many of the permanent exhibits should be completed late in 1995. Incorporated in the new theme, "America: 1908 to 1969," are personal facts about Lyndon Johnson: his birth on a farm near Stonewall, Texas, on August 27, 1908; his high school and college education; his experience as a teacher; and his job as an assistant to Richard Kleberg, a U.S. representative from Texas, in 1931. He met Claudia "Lady Bird" Taylor and married her on November 17, 1934. In 1935, at the age

Young LBJ was a boy from a little town in the Texas Hill Country who grew up to run for Congress.

of twenty-six, he was appointed administrator of the National Youth Administration by President Franklin D. Roosevelt.

It was during Roosevelt's presidency that twenty-nine-year-old Lyndon Johnson won a seat in the House of Representatives. In Congress he sought to secure flood control and electric power for the Hill Country of Central Texas. An ardent Roosevelt supporter, Johnson said on March 11, 1937: "I believe this District should have as its representative in Congress a man who is wholeheartedly committed to the support of the President's entire New Deal program. Let me make it plain that I am for every part of it."

By 1949, Johnson was in the Senate and quickly rose to Senate leadership. He became minority leader in 1953 and majority leader two years later. "Johnson's charms, his maneuvering ability and his genius for spotting political trends have given him a total command of the Senate matched by few majority leaders in history," reported *Time* magazine on May 27, 1957. Johnson exercised his leadership powers to pass the first civil rights bill since Reconstruction.

It was his track record as a forceful and effective leader in the Senate that put Johnson on Kennedy's successful presidential ticket in 1960. As vice president, Johnson served on the National Security Council, spearheaded a drive for minority employment opportunities, and headed the National Aeronautics and Space Council that recommended to President Kennedy a national commitment to a moon landing.

Few who were alive at the time will forget the assassination of President Kennedy on November 22, 1963, in Dallas, Texas, or how Lyndon Baines Johnson took the oath of office aboard the presidential airplane *Air Force One*. A museum exhibit captures the intensity of the moment in photographs of the Dallas motorcade, the slain president's casket, and Mrs. Kennedy's grief. Mrs. Johnson makes it even more personal with words from

LBJ made his mark in Congress, eventually rising to the position of senate majority leader before stepping down to become John F. Kennedy's vice president.

Vice President Johnson, flanked by his wife Lady Bird and Jacqueline Kennedy, is sworn in as president following the assassination of President Kennedy.

her White House diary. Then you are with President Johnson as he arrives at Andrews Air Force Base, the new leader of a shaken nation. Speaking to a joint session of Congress on November 27, 1963, five days after Kennedy's death, President Johnson said: "All I have I would have gladly given not to be standing here today."

An entirely different mood is established with the "Family Album" display. Photographs in a variety of frames are invitingly mounted on two wall-papered panels. Here you'll find the Johnson daughters—Lynda and Luci—their spouses, and their children. Nearby stands a White House limousine, a 1968 "Stretch" Lincoln flying the American and presidential flags, donated by the Ford Motor Company.

Lyndon B. Johnson was first, last and always a Texan.

Society's ills weighed heavily on this new president during his first days in office, and almost before he could begin to address them it was time for the 1964 campaign. Boasting his Texas heritage in a traditional hat, he won a term of his own. His vision for a "Great Society" spawned an outpouring of legislation on poverty, civil rights, the environment, the arts, health, and education.

"Two Americas" awaited him. A large transparency shows a birthday party with all the details of a Norman Rockwell scene, but behind it is a little girl, dressed in tattered clothing and looking out through a broken pane of glass. Her feet stand on a dirt floor; rats are part of her environment. The images are unforgettable.

President Lyndon Johnson signs legislation in 1965 establishing the Medicare program as former president Harry Truman, Bess Truman, Hubert Humphrey, and Lady Bird Johnson look on.

This overview of the 1960s also portrays the human tragedy of Vietnam. In a display titled "Rolling Thunder," life-sized soldiers stand before vivid photographs of the Vietnam conflict. There is a touching letter from a soldier who fought there, but there are also two letters from American citizens condemning the war. A memo from Secretary of Defense Robert S. McNamara informs President Johnson that to achieve success requires more troop involvement. By the end of 1968, the United States had sent 550,000 soldiers to South Vietnam. A 500-pound bomb draws attention to the escalation. The last line of the McNamara memo advises the president to expect as many as 2,000 casualties a week.

President Johnson had an intimate relationship with Congress. Here he converses with Senate leaders Mike Mansfield (left) and Everett McKinley Dirkson during the Vietnam War.

When the 1968 Democratic Convention begins, President Johnson is not a candidate for reelection. In a televised speech on March 31, 1968, he announced unilateral deescalation of the war in Vietnam and concluded with these words: "I shall not seek, and will not accept, the nomination of my party for another term as your president."[3] Two months later he ordered peace talks to begin in Paris between U.S. and North Vietnamese representatives.

Lighter moments also await visitors to the first floor of the exhibition hall. The culture of the age is present in reminders of the hippie era, fighter Mohammed Ali's championship, Dustin Hoffman's starring role in the hit movie *The Graduate*, astronauts walking on the moon, and Carol Channing singing "Hello Dolly."

Mounting the broad staircase to the second floor, you can see into the archival records area. Stacked behind glass are red boxes emblazoned with the gold presidential seal. Each level is dedicated to a separate topic. The White House Central Files, for example, are on the fourth level.

On the staircase landing you pause and read about how the library's holdings have aided scholars. Since 1971, research from the collection has produced or contributed to scores of doctoral dissertations, theses, books, and articles.

Beneath the stacks on the second floor, you encounter the impressive, fifty-foot-long mural "A Generation of Presidents." Photoengraved in magnesium, it was created by Naomi Savage and depicts the offices LBJ held and the chief executives under whom he served. At its center, engraved on a stone pillar, are four Johnson quotations. One reads: "I have followed the personal philosophy that I am a free man, an American, a public servant, and a member of my party, in that order always and only."

Within intimate kiosks on this floor are displays covering a variety of topics. There is a ten-minute video on LBJ's humor. The "America's Handiwork"

One of the most impressive sights in the museum is the great hall ending in a view of the archival stock area.

display has an eclectic assortment of gifts sent to the president: a quilt made of dress material from the wives of forty-eight governors, gavels, a white tie embroidered with the initials "LBJ", and Western memorabilia such as a Colt single-action army revolver and the sheet music to the song "The Yellow Rose of Texas." These gifts, Lady Bird Johnson observed, "come wrapped in love."

"The First Lady Theater" periodically offers a fifty-seven minute film titled *A Life: A Story of Lady Bird Johnson.* Lining one theater wall are wonderful photo prints of the official White House portraits of First Ladies. Many of Mrs. Johnson's White House activities are also featured in the theater as well as some of her philosophy. "You should work at the project," she said, "that will make your heart sing." To illustrate this saying, her work with Operation Head Start is presented. Also on display are the White House china and a gown Mrs. Johnson wore to the inaugural gala on January 18, 1965. For her efforts toward beautification of the environment, she received the Presidential Medal of Freedom from President Gerald Ford, which is also displayed here.

After leaving the White House, Mrs. Johnson continued her efforts to restore and preserve the beauty of America's rural and urban landscape by planting trees and flowers. In addition, she served on the Board of Regents of the University of Texas. She also became deeply involved in the development and building of the Johnson Library. "A Presidential Library," she said, "is many things."

It is the past: millions of documents ... all preserving some fragment of a time gone by. It is the present: a melding of library and museum, filled with voices of tourists, yet providing quiet retreats for scholars. Most of all it is the future: a place where the judgments of history will be made.

"American Political Memorabilia" is a lively exhibit with campaign songs playing, lights flashing, and an abundance of red, white, and blue in every imaginable combination of stars and stripes. Each president from George Washington in 1789 through Lyndon Johnson in 1968 is represented here. Most of the political memorabilia come from the Ralph C. Becker Collection, presented to President Johnson while he was still in the White House. One of the more unusual pieces is a giant Texas cowboy hat that was used in floor demonstrations at the Democratic national conventions of 1960 and 1964.

Another gallery, "Treasures from Around the World," contains gifts presented to the president, such as ceremonial swords from Saudi Arabia and Morocco; a horse and groom statue from Germany; ivory from Africa; a Chinese tomb sculpture from China; and the marble Portrait of a Youth, first century B.C., from Antonio Signi, president of the Italian Republic.

From the second floor you ascend by elevator to the eighth. The doors open on "Life in the White House." A replica of the president's Oval Office is to the left. A recorded message explains that every president since Theodore Roosevelt has occupied this office. The desk President Johnson used here dates back to his Senate days. On it papers are waiting. A three-screen television console and news service teletype convey this president's interest in having immediate access to the news. Then, accompanied by a recorded description from Lady Bird, the visitor views a panorama made from color transparencies of the executive mansion's public and private rooms.

Once back on the first floor, it seems appropriate to stop for a moment of reflection before "Beneficiaries of the Great Society," a large oil painting by Alfred Leslie. The painting depicts thirteen people, a cross-section of the Americans Lyndon Baines Johnson sought to help.

Ten minutes from the airport and off Interstate 35, the museum of the Lyndon Baines Johnson Library is open 9 A.M. to 5 P.M. daily except Christmas. Admission is free. The library is located at 2313 Red River Street, Austin, Texas 78705. Telephone: (512) 482-5279.

NOTES

1. *The Lyndon Baines Johnson Library & Museum: A Progress Report,* produced by the Lyndon Baines Johnson Foundation.

2. Ibid. Other direct quotations in this chapter were taken from this source or from written scripts prepared by the staff of the museum.

3. Quoted in "Lyndon Baines Johnson," *Funk & Wagnalls New Encyclopedia,* vol. 15 (New York: Funk & Wagnalls L.P., 1987), 9192.

CHAPTER 8

Richard Nixon

LIBRARY DEDICATED: JULY 19, 1990

YORBA LINDA, CALIFORNIA

Richard M. Nixon, a Republican, was elected to serve two terms (1969–1973,

1973–1977) in office. He resigned the presidency on August 9, 1974.

THE RICHARD NIXON LIBRARY and Birthplace is the only one of the presidential libraries to be totally operated with private funds. When it was opened to the public, the former president told those gathered for the dedication ceremony what they would find:

What you will see here, among other things, is a personal life—the influence of a strong family, of inspirational ministers, of great teachers. You will see a political life—running for Congress, running for the Senate, running for governor, running for president three times. And you will see the life of a great nation—77 years of it. A period in which we had unprecedented progress for the United States. And you will see great leaders—leaders who changed the world, who helped to make the world what we have today.[1]

The Nixon complex spans nine acres of the original twelve-acre citrus grove once worked by the president's parents, Frank and Hannah Nixon. As a reminder of the past, a small grove of citrus trees stands to the right of the main entrance.

Visitors climb gentle stairs to enter three low, sandstone-colored pavilions with red-tiled roofs. These adjoining pavilions border lush gardens and a 130-foot reflecting pool. The building, designed by Langdon Wilson Architecture & Planning of Newport Beach, California, is traditional and deliberately creates a welcoming instead of a monumental atmosphere.[2]

Inside, the lobby is an additional reminder of President Nixon's heritage. Its high-peaked ceiling mimics that of the Quaker meeting halls once attended by the Nixon family. Through a glass wall on the east side, you can see the reflecting pool and the farmhouse where Nixon was born. Beneath this expanse of glass is a time line display of the president's ancestors on the Milhous and Nixon sides of the family. The time line documents their connections to Yorba Linda and Whittier, California, where the family moved when Richard Nixon was nine years old. It is illustrated with photographs, letters, and artifacts such as an engraved first place medal for extemporaneous speaking that was given to the president in 1933 by the Southern California Speaking Conference. A gavel engraved "Duke Bar Association, Richard Nixon, President, 1936–7" also is displayed. The time line introduces Pat Ryan, who performed with Nixon in the community theater production of *The Dark Tower*. Their courtship and marriage were followed by years of separation when Nixon enlisted in the navy. These life experiences led to a career of political service.

An additional preparation for the main exhibit area is a film narrated by Richard Nixon, *Never Give Up: Richard Nixon in the Arena*. Shown within a 293-seat theater, it focuses on the theme of "comeback," ending with an overview of the president's postpresidential activities. After you exit the theater, you are brought back to the beginning of Nixon's career. A wall-sized

The entrance to Richard Nixon Library and Birthplace is accented by a lush fountain.

Museum windows overlook the 130 foot reflecting pool and the First Lady's Garden.

photograph shows the young Nixon family posed with bicycles beside the Tidal Basin in Washington, D.C. The famed cherry blossoms are in bloom—and the Nixons are on the "Road to the Presidency."

At age thirty-three, Richard Nixon launches his first political campaign, a successful run for the U.S. House of Representatives. A script reads: "The jubilation that he and Pat felt on election night was never again to be equalled in his political career." A photograph presents the House of Representatives in session, January 1947, with Nixon captioned as "the greenest congressman in town." That Eightieth Congress "had two freshman congressmen who went on to become president. One was Richard Nixon; the other, a twenty-nine year old Democrat from Massachusetts, who was John Kennedy."[3]

Then it is on to the Senate. Nixon enters the race on November 3, 1949. Visitors see a wood-paneled stationwagon with a "Nixon for Senator" sign on top. As two men stand listening, the candidate uses the tailgate as a platform from which to speak. The election's outcome is acknowledged with these words: "Your victory was the greatest good that can come to our country," wrote former president Herbert Hoover to the newly elected senator in 1950.

Service in the Senate from 1951 to 1953 had its peaks and valleys. "The Hiss-Chambers Case" display shows the chronology that put Senator Nixon in the newspaper headlines as he successfully worked to unveil the activities of communist spies within the United States. A quote from Gen. Dwight D. Eisenhower states: "The thing that most impressed me was that you not only got Hiss, but you got him fairly." This led to Eisenhower's selection of Nixon as his running mate in 1952 for the presidential campaign.

During the campaign Nixon was accused of maintaining an $18,000 slush fund while he was a senator. The exhibit titled "Reshaping the Vice Presidency" begins with excerpts from the candidate's famous rebuttal to these charges. Visitors watch five minutes of a black-and-white televised address to the nation on September 23, 1952. While Nixon reveals his family's financial status, a tense Patricia Nixon looks on. She hears her husband say: "I am not a quitter, and Pat is not a quitter," before declaring that the only gift they ever accepted was a black-and-white cocker spaniel puppy named "Checkers," and the only coat Pat Nixon owned was a "Republican cloth coat." The "Fund Crisis Speech" ends with a plea to the listeners to send telegrams advising him whether he should withdraw or continue his run for office. Near the television set are canvas bags brimming with Western Union telegrams.

Voters elected Eisenhower and Nixon in 1952 and reelected this ticket in 1956. Nixon became one of the most widely traveled vice presidents, with trips to Central and South America, Hungary, the Soviet Union, Poland, and Asia. He was the "first Vice President to assume a major role in the making of foreign policy, covering more that 150,000 miles." Maps, photographs, and gifts (such as an ivory and gold leg bracelet presented to him in Ghana in 1957) complete this display.

Then the 1960 presidential campaign begins. Paraphernalia from this era shows Nixon and his running mate, Henry Cabot Lodge, taking on John F. Kennedy and vice presidential candidate Lyndon Baines Johnson. Later Nixon commented, "Jack Kennedy and I were both in the peak years of our political energy, and we were contesting great issues in a watershed period of American life and history."[4]

Completing this display, a comfortable couch faces a vintage television set. On its screen is an excerpt from "The Great Debates," four exchanges between Nixon and Kennedy that captivated the voting public. Kennedy's election ended Nixon's early years in Washington, D.C. "I thought about the great experiences of the past fourteen years," Nixon said at the time. "Now all that was over, and I would be leaving Washington, which had been my home since I arrived as a young congressman in 1947. . . . I suddenly stopped short, struck by the thought that this was not the end—that someday I would be back here."[5]

This begins "The Wilderness Years, 1961–1967," and the family's return to California, where Nixon resumed the practice of law. At the urging of Mrs. Eisenhower, Nixon wrote *Six Crises,* a bestseller on his experiences as vice president. Also documented is Nixon's unsuccessful bid to become governor of California in 1962.

Nixon's faltering political career gets a fresh start with the 1968 campaign for the presidency. "Bring Us Together" is the title of the exhibit that introduces visitors to the top concerns of those days: the Vietnam War and the assassination of political leaders—in particular, Martin Luther King, Jr., and Robert Kennedy.

Banners, buttons, and more illustrate the theme of that Republican presidential campaign, "Nixon's the One!" He entered every state primary to demonstrate his ability to win the election. Maps and photographs show his extensive travel and the effort he made to best the Democratic opponents, then vice president Hubert Humphrey and Maine senator Edmund Muskie.

Next, step into the unique exhibit area titled "World Leaders" and rub elbows with the life-sized Charles de Gaulle of France, Konrad Adenauer of West Germany, Winston Churchill of Great Britain, Yoshida Shigeru of Japan, Anwar al-Sadat of Egypt, Golda Meir of Israel, Chou En-lai and Mao Tse-tung of China, and Nikita Khrushchev and Leonid Brezhnev of the Soviet Union. Seated or standing in conversation, all of the figures are made of plaster of paris and were dressed in real clothes before being sprayed with bronze-like epoxy. Standing among them, most visitors speak softly as though they are concerned about being overheard.

For those eager to learn more about these ten world leaders, there is a touch screen with information about each one. Two side walls are covered with display cases containing priceless gifts from around the globe. Courtesy of the National Archives, these treasures now belong to the American people. Flags from countries that the featured leaders represented are suspended overhead and a Nixon quote enhances the mood: "They are the leaders who have made a difference. Not because they wished it, but because they willed it."

Before leaving this area, visitors can look at a photograph of the U.S. Capitol on Inauguration Day, January 20, 1969, as Richard Nixon is sworn in as America's thirty-seventh president. The display case also holds the family Bible used in the ceremony and this message broadcast to the nation, "Let us have this as our goal: Where peace is unknown, make it welcome; where peace is fragile, make it strong; where peace is temporary, make it permanent."

President Nixon and Secretary General Leonid Brezhnev shake hands after the signing of the SALT I Agreement.

Moving into a gallery titled "A Structure of Peace," visitors discover displays dealing with the ending of the Vietnam War and the efforts that were required to expand a dialogue with China and the Soviet Union. The president's words read: "We are entering an era of negotiation. Let all nations know that during this administration our lines of communication will be open. We seek an open world—open to ideas, open to the exchange of goods and people—a world in which no people, great or small, will live in angry isolation."

One sign of appreciation is a Suzhou cat presented to the Nixons by Premier Chou En-lai during a second visit to China in 1976. This beautiful double-sided embroidery took years to complete as artisans split single threads of silk into slender filaments and wove them into the screen. Freestanding and elegantly mounted in an Oriental frame, the cat is exquisite on both sides.

Nearby is a pagoda and the July 15, 1971, announcement that President Nixon would visit China, a country that had not been recognized by the United States for more than twenty years. In February of 1972, he shook hands with Chou En-lai on Chinese soil and held talks with Communist leader Mao Tse-tung.

The Vietnam display, which reviews the history of this war, concludes with the peace agreement signed on January 27, 1973. The thrust to "end war, win peace" is illustrated with a television address by President Nixon on November 3, 1969. In this speech Nixon appealed to the "silent majority" of Americans for support of his policies to end the war. Standing before another vintage television set, visitors can listen to six minutes of this broadcast that generated 50,000 telegrams and 30,000 letters of support. A museum script reads: "The President's approval rating jumped eleven points, the biggest increase as a result of a Presidential speech in the history of the Gallup Poll—a milestone against which all other Presidential addresses are judged."

Another display covers the dramatic dinner on May 24, 1973, in honor of American prisoners of war—the largest state dinner ever held at the White House. During the evening, those gathered sang "God Bless America." The original song manuscript, presented to the president that night by composer Irving Berlin, is exhibited.

Next visitors encounter a graffiti-covered, twelve-foot-high section of the Berlin Wall, a visceral reminder of America's fight against communism. A

The first American president to travel to Communist China, Nixon's 1972 summit meeting in China was widely applauded and symbolized a new beginning for U.S.-Chinese relations. Here Nixon visits the Great Wall.

President Nixon nominated both Lewis F. Powell, Jr. (left), a Democrat, and William H. Rehnquist (right), a Republican, to the Supreme Court on October 21, 1971.

structure featuring Moscow "onion domes" is nearby. Beneath its "roof" is a history of many transactions with the Soviet Union: Summits I, II, and III plus the signing of the first Strategic Arms Limitation Treaty (SALT I) on May 26, 1972. In Moscow that year Nixon said: "We want to be remembered for our deeds . . . by the fact that we made the world a more peaceful one for all the people in the world."

Then it's on to a light-filled gallery titled "Pat Nixon: Ambassador of Goodwill." Beneath windows overlooking the "First Lady's Garden" is a time line that begins with her birth on March 16, 1912. It then takes viewers through her youth to graduation from the University of Southern California to a teaching position at Whittier Union High School. "I've decided that the only reason that I accepted the teaching job was destiny," she later explained. "Through it I met Dick in his own home town."

Family photographs document their marriage, work experiences, and the birth of their daughters, Tricia and Julie. Also documented are the travels of Pat Nixon, the most traveled First Lady in U.S. history. By the end of her White House years, she had visited seventy-eight countries and logged 108,000 miles, nearly 30,000 alone. One of her most poignant trips was to Peru to comfort the victims of an earthquake on May 31, 1970. Again her words and a photograph speak volumes: "I believe that even when people can't speak your language, they can tell if you have love in your heart."

At the end of this gallery hangs the Official White House portrait from 1972: Julie and David Eisenhower, the president and Mrs. Nixon, and Tricia and Edward Cox. The gallery also covers Mrs. Nixon's return to private life in San Clemente in 1974 and her stroke and recovery. In the final image she is pictured enjoying her grandchildren.

Leaving this area, one finds the "Lincoln Sitting Room," re-created because of President Nixon's fondness for it. Looking in you read: "It is the smallest room in the White House and my favorite." Furnishings include the brown chair and ottoman actually used by President Nixon.

Standing outside the sitting room, visitors see the president's handwritten pages, showing the evolution of a speech as it goes through numerous stages. Or they can step into "Prime Time Theatre," where sixteen seats are provided for the viewing of various film and video highlights from the Nixon years.

A more intimate look at life in the White House is presented through photos of social events and places visited: San Clemente, Camp David, and Key Biscayne. The "Gowns" display features Tricia Nixon Cox's wedding dress, Julie Nixon Eisenhower's bridal and bridesmaid gowns, and Pat Nixon's 1973 inaugural gown and a red coat worn during her 1972 China trip.

"Domestic Affairs" is the theme of one exhibit. Coverage ranges from the economy and energy issues of the time through the president's war on cancer, one of the initiatives of which he was most proud. Creating an upbeat and patriotic mood are numerous American flags and an 1823 engraved facsimile of the Declaration of Independence. A side gallery, "Gifts of the People," includes an autographed picture of the Elvis Presley family.

Then it's on to the "1972 Campaign" with Nixon and Spiro T. Agnew opposing George McGovern and Sargent Shriver. The Nixon team wins "four more years," the popular chant of his supporters, but he resigns from office after only two. Visitors approach a long, darkened corridor titled "Watergate: The Final Campaign." Your eye goes to the end where the former president is pictured waving goodbye to the nation on August 9, 1974.

Following his journey through the crisis, you can read the transcript or listen to the president's recorded conversation with his chief of staff, Bob Haldeman. This taped conversation became known as Watergate's smoking gun. The chronology of Watergate is reviewed through photographs of the people involved and descriptions of key events. The exhibit concludes with the president's thirty-seventh televised address to the nation on August 8, 1974, when he announced his resignation.

The "Presidential Forum" display summarizes Nixon's career as president. By using a touch screen, visitors can ask questions and receive video answers from the president. "In the Arena" provides information on what he accomplished after leaving office. He wrote several books, returned to China, and consulted with all subsequent U.S. presidents.

Exiting the Museum, one enters the formal garden surrounding the reflecting pool. It is only a short walk to Nixon's birthplace. Along the path you will discover the deep red blooms of the "Pat Nixon Rose" and her simply marked burial site. Following his death on April 22, 1994, Nixon was eulogized by President Bill Clinton, among others, and laid to rest beside her.

With the possibility of House impeachment looming, President Nixon announced his resignation in an emotional television address on August 8, 1974. His daughter Tricia is to his left.

Birthplace

In the small white clapboard farmhouse built by his father, Richard Milhous Nixon was born on January 9, 1913. In an audio program, he describes the house, its furnishings (including the piano on which as a boy he took lessons), and a host of memories. Standing in its entry hall, you hear in part: "As a young boy in Yorba Linda, I never thought of becoming President of the United States, or even entering politics. My goal was to become a railroad engineer. Sometimes at night I was awakened by the sound of a train whistle, and I would dream of the far-off places I wanted to visit someday."[6]

The Richard Nixon Library and Birthplace is located approximately twenty minutes from Orange County and fifty minutes from the Los Angeles In-

A walkway beside the reflecting pool leads to the modest farmhouse where America's thirty-seventh president was born.

ternational Airports. It is open Monday through Saturday from 10 A.M. to 5 P.M., Sundays from 11 A.M. to 5 P.M. except Thanksgiving and Christmas days. Schedule subject to change. Admission fee for visitors age eight and older. The address is 18001 Yorba Linda Boulevard, Yorba Linda, California 92686. Telephone: (714) 993-3393.

NOTES

1. Richard Nixon Library and Birthplace, excerpts of remarks from the dedication and opening ceremonies of the Richard Nixon Library and Birthplace on July 19, 1990, press release, August 1990, 2.

2. Leon Whiteson, "The Design: Unmonumental Library Reflects Nixon's Unpretentious Beginnings," *Los Angeles Times,* July 17, 1990, 12–13.

3. Script, Richard Nixon Library.

4. Ibid.

5. Ibid.

6. Richard Nixon Library and Birthplace, "Birthplace Audio" script, 1.

CHAPTER 9

Gerald R. Ford

MUSEUM DEDICATED: SEPTEMBER 18, 1981

GRAND RAPIDS, MICHIGAN

Vice President Gerald R. Ford, a Republican, was sworn into office on

August 9, 1974, following the resignation of President Richard M. Nixon,

and he completed the remainder of Nixon's term (1974–1977).

VISITING DOWNTOWN Grand Rapids, one finds the Gerald R. Ford Museum located on a six-acre plot in an attractive twenty-acre park complex along the west bank of the Grand River. The building is just a short walk from the site where Ford established his first political headquarters in 1948. What followed was twenty-five years of congressional service.

Approaching the sleek two-story museum, designed by Marvin DeWinter Associates of Grand Rapids, one sees the city where Jerry Ford grew up. It is unexpectedly reflected in the mirrored windows that form the outer walls of the building. The exterior is made even more impressive by a fountain, shooting forty feet into the air, and the contrasting calm of a 250-foot-long reflecting pool. Near the main entrance are two remarkable pieces: a graffiti-covered segment of the Berlin Wall, donated on the Museum's tenth anniversary, and a "Man in Space" sculpture by Judson Nelson.

Inside the front door is a spacious lobby, classically modern with an abundance of live plants. An inscription bears these words from President Ford's swearing-in ceremony on August 9, 1974, the day Nixon resigned.

You have not elected me as your President by your ballots and so I ask you to confirm me as your President with your prayers.... I have not sought this enormous responsibility, but I will not shirk it.... Our Constitution works; our great republic is a government of laws and not of men. Here the people rule.... God helping me, I will not let you down.[1]

Reflecting the enormity of the job, a presidential seal—carved from limestone and measuring a massive eleven feet in diameter—is mounted where visitors can see it upon entering the lobby. It is bathed in gold light.

Tours generally begin with a viewing of the twenty-eight-minute film *Gerald R. Ford: The Presidency Restored*, which profiles his exciting career of

The Ah-Nab-Awen Bicentennial Park—a memorial to the tribes who once inhabited west Michigan—fronts and separates the Gerald R. Ford Museum from the Grand River.

public service. As the thirty-eighth president of the United States, he inherited the office during troubled times and successfully labored to restore calm and confidence in the nation's democratic process.

Primed to learn more about this man, you enter the museum and encounter a chronological display, "Boyhood and Beyond." You learn that Gerald R. Ford, Jr., was born Leslie L. King, Jr., on July 14, 1913. Soon after his birth, his mother, Dorothy, took her son and fled Omaha and an abusive husband. With help from her parents, she resettled in Grand Rapids, where she met and married Gerald R. Ford. At the age of twenty-two, Leslie L. King, Jr., legally changed his name to Gerald R. Ford, Jr., in honor of the man who raised him.[2]

Visitors to the exhibit learn about the Ford family (Gerald had three half-brothers) and about a youngster's typical activities: scouting, sports, and school. As a young man Ford became an Eagle Scout, was voted most popular senior in high school, and attended the University of Michigan where he played football. Coaching football and freshman boxing at Yale University helped him pay off his debts and save money before attending Yale Law School to earn his degree. Following graduation in 1941, he opened a law office in Grand Rapids with a friend, Philip Buchen. But before they had time to firmly establish themselves, World War II interfered. "The Navy Years" are shown through photographs and documents relating to Ensign Ford's exciting tour aboard the USS *Monterey.* Lieutenant Commander Ford's officer uniform is part of the display.

Nineteen forty-eight was another busy year for Ford as he opened his first campaign for the U.S. House of Representatives. In *Time and Chance: Gerald Ford's Appointment with History,* biographer James Cannon writes: "For his campaign office, Ford deliberately chose both a symbol and a site. To emphasize his World War II service, he rented a Navy surplus Quonset hut and painted it red, white and blue; then he set it up in the parking lot of Wurzburg's downtown department store, just below the office window of his political nemesis, Frank McKay."[3] Ford's Quonset hut headquarters is replicated here with all the furnishings and flyers of a shoestring volunteer operation.

Then it's on to the "Romance and Marriage" exhibit. One month after winning the Republican primary, Gerald R. Ford, Jr., married Betty Bloomer

Warren in Grand Rapids on October 15, 1948. The bride's wedding hat of sapphire blue satin, her garter, and a lucky penny can be seen.

Ford won the general election and served in the U.S. House from 1949 to 1973. In 1965 he was elected House Minority Leader. In this role Representative Ford is seen and heard in a six-minute video. Expanding further on this theme of his congressional years is a diagram of how a bill becomes law. An important part of his job on the Hill was winning support for his party's legislation. Ford's desk as it was furnished the day Nixon resigned is also recreated here. Views of the U.S. Capitol provide an additional glimpse of this heady environment.

On October 10, 1973, Vice President Spiro Agnew resigned, and President Nixon nominated Gerald Ford to succeed Agnew as vice president. Twenty-five years of preparation and political experience led to Ford's selection. The Senate confirmation hearings and Ford's thoughts on the office are provided in a five-minute video.

Pressure builds and Watergate leads to the resignation of President Nixon. A copy of his resignation letter, written on White House stationery and addressed to Secretary of State Henry Kissinger, is displayed near the Twenty-fifth Amendment to the Constitution ("Whenever there is a vacancy in the office of the Vice President, the President shall nominate a Vice President who shall take office upon confirmation by a majority vote of both Houses of Congress").[4] A tally sheet documents Ford's overwhelming confirmation vote in the House and Senate. The Bible upon which he swore the presidential oath is on display and open to Proverbs 3: "Trust in the Lord with all thine heart; and lean not unto thine own understanding. In all ways acknowledge Him, and He shall direct thy paths."

The "White House Model" exhibit contains a floor plan of the ceremonial rooms, staff offices, and family quarters. Two of the Fords' four children—

Steve and Susan—lived with their parents in the White House. The exhibit offers an outside/inside look at every president's home.

Soon you arrive at possibly the most popular exhibit in the Museum, a full-scale replica of the Oval Office. Via audiotape, President Ford relates some of his experiences as commander in chief. He describes both the exhilaration and the burdens this position entails. While you scan the room, perhaps noting the president's pipe rack beside his desk or the wheel of the USS *Mayaguez,* you hear:

The first time I walked into the Oval Office as a young member of the Congress, it scared me, particularly when you walk in to meet a President. I was awe-struck. I'll never forget it. On the other hand, after you've been President and walk in there every day, it becomes a workshop where you have papers flowing in, decisions that have to be made, orders that flow out. It's where tremendous decisions are made. Where the President in the quiet must decide yes or no on matters that involve the security and the safety and the prosperity of our land. The Oval Office is more than a symbol. It's a true seat of power in the Executive Branch of our Government. It is, without a question of doubt, the most important single room in our country and all who occupy it are very, very fortunate.[5]

No president serves alone. The next exhibit profiles Nelson Rockefeller, the second vice president, after Ford, to be appointed under the Twenty-fifth Amendment. During his short term, he chaired a commission on the CIA and led a domestic policy study group.

Details of Ford's pardon of former president Nixon are on exhibit. First come the documents establishing the president's authority to offer a pardon, then Ford's pardon message, which reads in part: "But it is not the ultimate fate of Richard Nixon that most concerns me—though surely it deeply troubles every *decent* and *compassionate* person. My concern is the immediate future of this great country." Ford pardoned Nixon for all federal crimes he might have committed in office. Letters from American citizens, both pro and con the pardon, end this display.

One of his many duties, President Ford takes questions from the White House press corps.

The heavy domestic issues facing this president during his short term are explained in another exhibit. These included an economic recession, refugee resettlement, and the somewhat unpopular clemency for Vietnam draft dodgers. Photographs, documents, and cartoons illustrate America's many views.

For "Three Days of the Presidency," Ford was consumed by the Cambodian seizure of the USS *Mayaguez*. Swift military action resulted in the recovery of the ship and its crew, but fifteen U.S. Marines were killed, three were missing in action, and fifty were wounded. In addition, twenty-three air force security troops were killed when their helicopter crashed during support operations. President Ford's actions during the crisis are documented through memos, photographs, and audiotape.

"I am indebted to no man, and to only one woman—my dear wife—as I begin this very difficult job," President Ford stated during his swearing-in ceremony.[6] As visitors to "The First Lady" gallery learn, Betty Ford was far from idle during the White House years. The Equal Rights Amendment was a key issue for her, and she was highly involved with promoting it, even though it failed to be ratified. An ERA flag, designed to be flown from her limousine, was presented to Mrs. Ford by friends on the White House staff. Red and white calico bloomers, a good-natured reference to her maiden name, are centered on blue satin. Circling the bloomers are the words: "DON'T TREAD ON ME—E.R.A." Completing this exhibit is a changing display of dresses Mrs. Ford wore as First Lady.

Domestic issues were not the only ones requiring President Ford's well-honed leadership skills. Committed to continuing Nixon's active foreign policy, he attended SALT talks, the Helsinki Conference, the 1974 Economic Summit, the signing of the Sinai Accord, and the 1975 NATO Summit. But even the First Family requires time out. A wall opposite the "Foreign Affairs" gallery shows the President and Mrs. Ford relaxing with their dog Liberty at the presidential retreat, Camp David.

Foreign affairs is not all work. The state visits of foreign leaders offer many opportunities to entertain. In the "State Visits" gallery you see the round table setting, preferred by Mrs. Ford, for a state dinner with President Giscard d'Estaing of France. She often used antique weathervanes, Indian baskets, historic silver pieces, and other Americana combined with flowers instead of standard floral arrangements. This guest list included popular actor Clint Eastwood and dance pioneer Martha Graham, with whom Mrs. Ford once studied. Among the state gifts on display is the Omani falcon, given to President Ford by the Sultan of Oman. Made of solid gold with a diamond crest, the bird rests in a silver tree.

Quilts patterned with symbols that show pride, patriotism, and a love of country were sent to President Ford by citizens to mark America's Bicentennial Anniversary.

America marked its two hundredth birthday during the Ford administration. Visitors can relive the festivities by watching *An American Celebration: the Bicentennial,* an award-winning fifteen-minute slide show containing photographs by nearly 100 photographers. Displayed near the amphitheater is a small sample of bicentennial gifts. One of the most amusing, made by CeEl Rosso, is a standing papier maché caricature of President Ford as a Revolutionary War soldier. The head is oversized. His belly is slightly rounded, and his shoes have seen better days.

The last exhibit most visitors see is the "1976 Campaign." Incumbent Gerald Ford wins the Republican nomination over challenger Ronald Reagan

Flanked by Secret Service agents as he campaigns, President Ford waves to a friendly crowd.

and goes on to campaign against Jimmy Carter. A five-minute video shows a segment of their televised debate. When the general election is held, however, Jimmy Carter wins. In his inaugural address President Carter acknowledged President Ford's greatest accomplishment when he said: "For myself and for our Nation, I want to thank my predecessor for all he has done to heal our land."[7]

The Gerald R. Ford Library

In a unique separation of the presidential museum and library functions, the museum's sister building, The Gerald R. Ford Library, is located in Ann Arbor on the campus of President Ford's alma mater, the University of Michigan. Built adjacent to the Bentley Library (Michigan Historical Collections), it was designed by the same architects—Jickling, Lyman and Powell

President Ford was the first president to separate the two major functions associated with presidential libraries. His archives are located in the Gerald R. Ford Library on the campus of his alma mater, the University of Michigan. His museum is in Grand Rapids, his old congressional district.

Associates of Birmingham, Michigan. This low-lying, two-story structure is made of pale red brick and bronze-tinted glass. Inside, a two-story lobby opens onto an outdoor plaza. Through a window wall, visitors can watch the hypnotic movement of two large stainless steel triangles, a kinetic sculpture by George Rickey.[8] (For additional information on the library, see the chapter on library resources.)

The Gerald R. Ford Museum is open Monday through Saturday, 9:00 A.M. to 4:45 P.M., and Sunday, noon to 4:45 P.M. Admission fee for those sixteen and older. It is located at 303 Pearl Street, N.W., Grand Rapids, Michigan 49504. Telephone: (616) 451-9263.

NOTES

1. Gerald R. Ford Museum, *Gerald R. Ford Museum, Grand Rapids, Michigan,* four-color brochure.

2. James Cannon, *Time and Chance: Gerald Ford's Appointment with History* (New York: HarperCollins, 1994), 22.

3. Cannon, *Time and Chance,* 49.

4. "Constitution of the United States," *Funk and Wagnalls New Encyclopedia,* vol. 7 (New York: Funk and Wagnalls L. P., 1971), 167.

5. "Oval Office Tape," written transcript, Gerald R. Ford Library, Grand Rapids, Michigan.

6. *Ford Museum,* 19.

7. Ibid., 20. For more information about the Gerald R. Ford Museum, see the one-page sheet, *Facts about the Gerald R. Ford Museum,* distributed by the Library. See also the seven-page handout titled *The Gerald R. Ford Library and Museum,* also distributed by the Library.

8. *Ford Library History,* nine pages of information produced by Gerald R. Ford Library, January 1990.

CHAPTER 10

Jimmy Carter

LIBRARY DEDICATED: OCTOBER 1, 1986
ATLANTA, GEORGIA

Jimmy Carter, a Democrat, became president on January 20, 1977,

and served one term (1977–1981).

I N T H E I R B O O K , *Everything to Gain,* Jimmy and Rosalynn Carter enthusiastically describe the location of the Carter Presidential Center that includes the Jimmy Carter Library: "We had found the perfect site for it in the heart of Atlanta—thirty acres located between downtown and Emory University, only a short distance from each. It is an area that was cleared for a highway intersection in the early seventies, but the highway was never built. We felt very fortunate. . . ."[1] Visitors soon discover why.

To reach the library, you leave Atlanta's urban claims behind and climb upward. The Center's grounds have a retreat-like atmosphere. Five interconnected round buildings blend into a hill from which Gen. William Tecumseh Sherman once watched the battle of Atlanta. Today it offers an impressive, panoramic view of the city's skyline.

The Carters have described the Center's architecture as "understated in design and beautiful." Visitors see buildings that appear futuristic but have classical columns. Two small lakes separate the heavily visited Library from the remaining buildings.

Placed between the lakes and extending to the Museum's entrance is a unique Japanese garden designed by Kinsaku Nakane. Seven tons of stone were used to create nineteen feet of waterfalls and a landscape filled with azaleas and other native plants. The scene is most spectacular when all the flowers are in bloom.

Passing the garden, visitors push through the doors and enter the library's museum. Designed as a teaching center, its primary focus is the institution of the presidency, the aspirations and expectations of the American people about their president, and the development and continuity of the office. Within the context of this theme, the career and presidency of Jimmy Carter

Visitors to the Jimmy Carter Library may enjoy a stroll around the Carter Center grounds. It contains a Japanese garden with an imitation landscape of deep mountains and secluded valleys, including two symbolic waterfalls.

are presented. A thirty-minute feature film, not on the life of Jimmy Carter but on the changing role of the president during this century, is narrated by Cliff Robertson. Carter offers comments on some of his experiences as president.

Outside the theater, a floor-to-ceiling exhibit titled "The 20th Century Presidency" expands upon the film's theme. A portrait of each president, beginning with Theodore Roosevelt (1901–1909) and continuing through Jimmy Carter (1977–1981), is featured as well as each president's predominant role, such as conservationist, national leader, and reformer. Above President Carter's name, one reads "peacemaker/protector of human rights." A plaque reads:

On September 7, 1977, President Carter and Panamanian leader Brig. Gen. Omar Torrijos Herrera signed the treaty that transferred control of the Panama Canal to Panama after the year 2000.

As President, Carter fulfilled campaign promises to develop a national energy program, protect the nation's natural resources and aid education.

Carter gained world-wide recognition for his sensitive negotiations on the Panama Canal treaties and his role in achieving an Egypt-Israeli Treaty of Peace. He continued nuclear arms talks with the Soviet Union and strengthened ties with the People's Republic of China.

The nation and the world responded to Jimmy Carter's call for human rights. His struggle to make the idea of human rights a reality refreshed America's spirit and reminded the world of humanity's common bond.

Having learned the major accomplishments of the Carter administration, visitors move on to the next stop, his White House Oval Office. The desk top is relatively free of clutter. Easily identified are a glass donkey, an in-basket, a reproduction of President Harry S. Truman's "The Buck Stops Here" sign, and a Bible. A Truman bust stands against a wall. With the push of a button, President Carter speaks, describing his daily routine. A visual display provides President Carter's own historic overview:

The President of the United States occupies one of the most powerful of all political offices and, as the leader of our nation, exerts tremendous influence in world affairs. The 38 Presidents who preceded me placed their singular stamp on the office as they met the challenges of history.

I too, confronted many long-standing and historic issues, and responded to them in light of the prevailing times. I invite you to consider some of these decisions as you visit with us today, and to ask yourselves what importance they have—not only for your individual lives but for our nation and the world. Then come to the "Town Meeting" to discuss them with me.

It was a supreme honor for me to serve as President of our great country.

During his presidency, Jimmy Carter played a major role in the peace negotiations between Egypt and Israel. Pictured in a three-way handshake at the Egyptian-Israeli Peace Treaty signing agreement in 1979 are Egyptian President Anwar al-Sadat, Carter, and Israeli Prime Minister Menachem Begin.

President Carter meets with Jody Powell, his press secretary (left), and Hamilton Jordan, his White House chief of staff.

The "Town Meeting" is an interactive video display in the center of the museum. Visitors are invited to enter a dialogue with President Carter, who will answer questions ranging from "What did Amy do all day at the White House?" to "Why did you choose to go to Camp David with Sadat and Begin?" Through a nearby window you can see a portion of the presidential archives that includes a staggering 27 million pages of documents, 1.5 million photographs, and 40,000 objects.

Not far from the "Town Meeting" video display is a photograph of President Carter, Rosalynn Carter, and their daughter Amy walking down Pennsylvania Avenue on Inauguration Day, January 20, 1977. Nearby is an arch-

On Inauguration Day, Jimmy Carter strolled down Pennsylvania Avenue with his wife and daughter, signaling his democratic approach to the office of president.

way decorated with photographs of men, women, and children from around the world. The archway symbolizes the basic human rights of each citizen, among them the freedom of speech, self-government, and safe passage. President Carter stressed the issue of human rights in his inaugural address:

Our commitment to human rights must be absolute, ... the powerful must not persecute the weak, and human dignity must be enhanced.... The world itself is now dominated by a new spirit. People ... are craving, and now demanding their place in the sun—not just for the benefit of their own physical condition, but for basic human rights.... Because we are free, we can never be indifferent to the fate of freedom elsewhere.

A very popular exhibit with a lighter touch is "More Than Fabric and Frills: First Lady Gown Reproductions." There are photographs and reproductions of gowns worn by First Ladies. Naturally the eye seeks out Eleanor Rosalynn Smith Carter. The script explains that she "wore the same gown for the 1977 inaugural balls that she had worn at the 1971 inauguration of her husband as governor of Georgia. The gown is blue-silk chiffon, with full skirt and sleeves and is trimmed at waist and waistband with gold braid. A matching full-length sleeveless coat is woven with blue and gold-colored threads."

The "Early Life" exhibit quickly introduces visitors to Carter's family members and places him in Plains, Georgia, both as a farmer and a public servant. Documented along the way are his education, enrollment in the U.S. Naval Academy, and career as a naval officer. One photograph shows his fiancée, Rosalynn, and his mother, Miss Lillian, pinning on his ensign shoulder bars.

Major issues during Carter's presidency are depicted in wedge-shaped displays titled the "Campaign Room," "Panama Canal," "Middle East Peace," "Arms Control," "China," "Iran," and "Our Future." Particularly affecting are

Pictured on their wedding day, Jimmy and Rosalynn Carter were married July 7, 1946.

the president's handwritten notes to Egypt's president Anwar al-Sadat and Israel's prime minister Menachem Begin. These letters, signed "Your Friend, Jimmy Carter," led to the Camp David Accords.

Rosalynn Carter's role as First Lady is spotlighted with a photo collage, "Partner of the President." She is shown at home and abroad in Latin America as the president's representative. Her role as a mental health advocate and her interest in the welfare of senior citizens are featured. This display points out that largely due to her efforts, the president's Commission on Mental Health was established, the Mental Health Systems Act of 1980 was passed, and the Office of Prevention at the National Institute of Mental Health was formed. It is an impressive record.

The Museum tour almost complete, visitors are treated to an elegant display of a dinner table setting from the Carter White House and gifts of state. One of the most unusual gifts is a portrait of Jimmy Carter by Mexican artist Octavio Ocampo. It is composed of national and personal icons such as flags, skyscrapers, trucks, ships, an eagle in flight, and the Statue of Liberty.

The Carter Presidential Center

At the dedication of the Jimmy Carter Library, President Carter said, "I want the Carter Presidential Center to be a great resource for the people of Georgia, the Nation and the world and an expression of my gratitude for having been able to serve." The Center houses the Task Force for Child Survival, Global 2000, and the Carter Center of Emory University. These offices are not open to the general public. Projects include international conflict resolution, African governance, human rights, and domestic and international health policy.

Approximately fifteen miles from Atlanta's Hartsfield International Airport and three miles from downtown (exit 96 off Interstate 75/85), the Jimmy Carter Library is open Monday through Saturday, 9:00 A.M. to 4:45 P.M., and Sunday, noon to 4:45 P.M. except Thanksgiving, Christmas, and New Year's Day. Admission fee for those sixteen and older. It is located at One Copenhill Avenue, Atlanta, Georgia 30307. Telephone: (404) 331-0296.

1. Jimmy and Rosalynn Carter, *Everything to Gain: Making the Most of the Rest of Your Life* (New York: Random House, 1987), 29, 134–135. All other quotations in the chapter are from Museum scripts.

CHAPTER 11

Ronald Reagan

LIBRARY DEDICATED: NOVEMBER 4, 1991

SIMI VALLEY, CALIFORNIA

Ronald Reagan, a Republican, was sworn into office on January 20, 1981,

and completed two terms as president (1981–1985, 1985–1989).

T<small>RAVELING INTERSTATES</small> and freeways, visitors to the Reagan Library leave the bustling cities of Los Angeles, Santa Barbara, and Pasadena behind to reach Simi Valley. Presidential Drive leads to an exclusive 100-acre tract of unincorporated and undeveloped California foothills. Donated by the development partnership of Blakey-Swartz, it offers breathtaking views of the surrounding mountains—rugged Western landscape especially admired by President and Mrs. Reagan.

Approaching from the parking lot, you look down upon the red-tiled roof of a low, rambling Spanish-missionary-style building, the newest and the largest of the presidential libraries. Designed by the architectural firm of Stubbins Associates, it makes extensive use of redwood and adobe tile, and its 153,000 square feet are constructed around a central courtyard.

It was here that five presidents—then-president George Bush and former presidents Ronald Reagan, Jimmy Carter, Gerald Ford, and Richard Nixon—gathered on Dedication Day, November 4, 1991. "The doors of this Library are open now and all are welcome," Reagan told the assembled guests. "The judgement of history is left to you—the people. I have no fears of that, for we have done our best. And so I say, come and learn from it."[1]

On that quest you enter the museum lobby where high ceilings and an expanse of glass bring the outdoors in. On the rich, wood-paneled walls of the "Hall of Presidents," you can read the name of every past president of the United States. This dignified entry space has been designed to place Reagan's presidency in its historical context.[2]

Passing through the "Hall of Presidents," you enter the auditorium to view a documentary film on Reagan's life up to and during the presidency. You exit, eager to learn more, and immediately enter "The Early Years

The entrance and the grounds of the Ronald Reagan Presidential Library are landscaped with plants and trees native to California. The building surrounds a central courtyard and fountain.

Gerald Ford, Richard Nixon, George Bush, Ronald Reagan, and Jimmy Carter stand in a replica of the Oval Office during the dedication of Reagan's presidential library on November 4, 1991, while Bush was still president.

Gallery: Growing Up in the Heart of America." The living room from Reagan's boyhood home has been re-created here, and you read about what Reagan learned from his Midwestern upbringing:

I saw the unyielding spirit and determination of a people who were willing to pay the tremendous price that is sometimes needed to protect our freedom... people who wouldn't give up, even in the face of overwhelming obstacles. Those people taught me faith, self-reliance, tolerance and belief in self and country—values I have carried with me throughout my life.

Underscoring these values are memorabilia and photographs from Reagan's birth on February 6, 1911, through his career in Hollywood. You see the Reagan family (parents and his brother Neil); Reagan as a Dixon High School football player; and Reagan as a member of the swim team at Eureka College, where his interests were "dramatics, athletics and politics." Following graduation, he became a radio sports announcer in Iowa. Eventually, he moved to Hollywood, where he tried out for the movies—and made it when he signed a contract with Warner Brothers in 1937. His height of 6'1" and his weight of 175 pounds are documented as are his simple tastes.

This area offers one of the most intimate encounters with Reagan in the museum. You are brought up short by his voice, which describes key events in his early years. The seven summers he worked as a lifeguard made a life-long impression on him. Of paramount importance, he explains, are the lives he was privileged to save—seventy-seven in all.

This gallery ends with the "Hollywood Wall," a collection of film scenes and posters. It is noted that Ronald Reagan made fifty-three films. His two favorite roles were those of Drake McHugh in *King's Row* and George Gipp in *Knute Rockne*. In 1957 he and his wife, Nancy Davis Reagan, co-starred with Arthur Franz in *Hellcats of the Navy*. The Museum's only picture of Reagan's first wife, Jane Wyman, is also found here.

Reagan's movie career was interrupted by World War II. He served his time in the army making training films. Following discharge, he was unemployed for several months. During this period, he occupied himself by making model ships, drawing plans for his projects, and carving them from wood. Samples of his craftsmanship are on display.

Then it's on to the "Early Years Gallery: Road to the Presidency." Reagan's growing leadership abilities are conveyed with broad strokes in a video titled *Political Milestones*. Viewers learn about the political themes and conservative ideas that eventually gained him the presidency. His postwar movie career is quickly covered, and mention is made of his employment for eight years (1954–1962) as a public relations speaker for the General Electric Company.

Detailed exhibits cover Reagan's entry into politics—as president of the Screen Actors Guild (1947–1952, 1959–1960), as a supporter of Barry Goldwater's unsuccessful presidential campaign in 1964, and as governor of California (1967–1971, 1971–1975). Accomplishments during his two gubernatorial terms are noted, especially a $554 million surplus in revenue that was returned to the voters. His unsuccessful campaign to become the Republican presidential candidate in 1976 is addressed as well as the 1980 primary that led to his election. A wall of newspaper headlines proclaims Reagan's jubilant victory.

"The World in 1980 Gallery" examines the world Reagan inherited upon taking office. With American hostages being held in Iran, America's morale was low. The Soviet Union was the enemy, and the American economy was recessionary. Changes had to be made.

"The Presidency: Prosperity Gallery" sounds a theme originally heard when Reagan was governor of California, that of economic recovery. This is portrayed in a video, *The American Miracle: Economic Recovery in the Reagan*

In his 1988 State of the Union address, President Reagan derided Congress's last-minute passage of 3,296 pages of budget reconciliation and government appropriations.

Years. In sharp contrast, another video covers John Hinckley's attempt to assassinate President Reagan on March 30, 1981, two months and ten days after his election. Seriously wounded, Reagan makes a remarkable recovery. He runs for reelection in 1984 and wins. A large photo panel and map show his state-by-state victory. "The Reagan Administration" exhibit captures this photogenic president with Vice President George Bush and the Reagan Cabinet.

Leaving "Prosperity Gallery," you come upon the "Head of State Gifts Pavilion." Two thousand treasures from around the world are displayed on a rotating basis. A ruby tie tack and a mosaic cat with diamond eyes from Pakistan are among these treasures, which belong not to the president to whom they were given but to the people of the United States.

"The Presidency: Peace and Freedom Gallery" chronicles Reagan's major foreign policy achievements and ends with a media presentation entitled *Legacy.* In the gallery a "Peace through Strength" time line documents his efforts to strengthen the nation's defenses while negotiating for peace. This resulted in a treaty governing the use of intermediate-range nuclear forces (INF). Letters that were exchanged by President Reagan and Soviet leaders reveal what Reagan was trying to accomplish. This display includes a facsimile of the INF Treaty, the original pen used to sign it, a fragment of a destroyed Soviet missile, and these words by President Reagan: "...a nuclear war cannot be won and must never be fought."

The "World Leaders Wall" features President Reagan meeting with foreign heads of state. It is a good place to pause before studying the "Freedom and Democracy" time line, which documents President Reagan's support for those seeking freedom around the world and includes coverage of what has come to be called the Iran/Contra affair. Fred Otnes's photo collage of images and headlines testifies to the tremendous public response to this presi-

President Reagan held four summit meetings with Soviet leader Mikhail Gorbachev. These meetings led to the signing of Missile Agreements in Moscow and Washington, D.C.

dent's dogged efforts to promote peace and fight communism. Continuing the theme of this gallery is the video *Peace and Freedom: Foreign Policy in the Reagan Years.* Thirteen glass showcases (vitrines) display the names and stories of dissidents who had President Reagan as an advocate in their struggle for freedom. As a backdrop to these vitrines is a wall of names of dissidents who actually won their freedom during the Reagan years. Also listed are an impressive number of countries that became "substantially more free" by the end of Reagan's administration.

"Legacy Video Theater" offers a three-screen panoramic video that addresses the rise of communism, the end of the Cold War, and President Reagan's legacy of hope. It is a dramatic and impressionistic presentation.

Always a popular exhibit, the "Oval Office Replica" comes next. A sense of order reigns here. And associated with the Oval Office is the "Life in the

White House Gallery," which documents the private lives and public duties of the First Family. The visitor comes away with a sense of the Reagans' experiences in the White House, both typical days and days of crises. Gifts to President Reagan from the American people are also on exhibit.

One cannot fully understand this president without visiting "The First Lady's Gallery." It covers Nancy Davis Reagan's childhood, Hollywood career, and life as a wife, mother, and political partner. During Reagan's presidency, she became widely known for the Foster Grandparents program, and the Just Say No drug program. Both are highlighted in photographs, memorabilia, and awards she received. Included is the video *Nancy Reagan: A Personal Portrait.*

President Reagan met with Justice Sandra Day O'Connor in 1981. His nominee to the U.S. Supreme Court, O'Connor was sworn in on September 25, 1981, the first woman to be appointed to this position.

Whether delivering a speech on the campaign trail or riding a horse at Camp David, President Reagan's message to the American people conveyed optimism and confidence.

President and Nancy Reagan spent most weekends at Camp David, the presidential retreat. Walking the grounds with them is the retreat's commanding officer, James Broaddus.

Before exiting you can step into the "Meet President Reagan Interactive Video Theater." Here is one more opportunity to glean more about our fortieth president by accessing thematic topics.

Returning to the lobby, visitors are drawn to the panoramic scene outside. Erected at the edge of that scene is an authentic section of the Berlin Wall. The sections of the wall in other presidential libraries are in grim colors, but this section is painted in vivid shades of blue, green, and rose. Flowers and a magnificent butterfly cover the wall, which is 9.5 feet tall, 3.5 feet wide, and weighs 6,338 pounds. A nearby marker carries President Reagan's words dated October, 1983: "...to every person trapped in tyranny...our message must be: Your struggle is our struggle, your dream is our dream, and some-day you, too, will be free."

Located at 40 Presidential Drive, Simi Valley, California, the Ronald Reagan Library is open daily except Thanksgiving, Christmas, and New Year's Day. Hours are Monday through Saturday, 10 A.M. to 5 P.M., and Sunday, noon to 5 P.M. Admission fee for ages sixteen and older. For general information about the library, call (805) 522-8444.

NOTES

1. *Ronald Reagan Presidential Library,* color pamphlet published by the Ronald Reagan Presidential Library, Simi Valley, Calif.

2. For background information, see the four-page *Fact Sheet* distributed by the Ronald Reagan Presidential Library. See also *Reagan Library Exhibits: An Overview,* seven pages of information supplied by the Library.

CHAPTER 12

George Bush

LIBRARY UNDER CONSTRUCTION
COLLEGE STATION, TEXAS

George Bush, a Republican, was sworn into office on January 20, 1989,

and served one term (1989–1993).

O N   N O V E M B E R 30, 1994, a groundbreaking ceremony was held in College Station, Texas, the future site of the George Bush Presidential
Library Center. Located on ninety park-like acres of the Texas A&M University campus, the Presidential Library Center will include a museum,
archives, auditoria, and administrative offices and space for university programs. Visitors will enter the Texas granite and limestone structure, designed
by CRSS Architects, Inc., through a semicircular glass rotunda. In the middle
of the two wings—a one-story exhibition wing and a three-story archival
wing—will be a fifty-foot-high lobby crowned by a skylight rotunda.[1]

President Bush has said,

In this presidential library you will find documentation for some of the most revolutionary changes that the world has ever seen take place. Whether it is the peace
talks . . . or whether it is the unification in Germany . . . whether it is the decline
and fall of the Soviet Empire . . . whether it is the historic precedence-setting coalition for Desert Storm. All of that will be reflected with accurate detail in the library for scholars to make their own conclusions.[2]

The National Archives will operate the Presidential Library and Museum
and Texas A&M University will operate the adjacent university and shared-
use facilities.

The Library-Museum

The library-museum will chronicle not only Bush's presidency but also
his long career in public service: U.S. representative (1967–1971), U.S. ambassador to the United Nations (1971–1972), chairman of the Republican National Committee (1973–1974), chief of the U.S. Liaison Office in Peking
(1974–1975), and vice president (1981–1989). Particularly skillful in foreign
policy, President Bush is recognized around the globe for his successful mar-

An architect's rendering shows a central feature of the George Bush Presidential Library, the rotunda.

shaling of a thirty-nation coalition to oppose Iraq's invasion of Kuwait in August 1990. The United States' resulting military operation was called Desert Storm.

One of the unique displays planned for the library-museum is a re-creation of President Bush's office at Camp David. Here in his presidential retreat President Bush met informally with foreign dignitaries and made some of the most difficult decisions of his presidency.

"In our library, you're going to be able to see, touch and feel various

President Bush made frequent trips to his home in Kennebunkport, Maine. Whether in or out of the White House, he still had to deal with the issues of the day. He is shown holding an impromptu meeting with the ever-present press corps.

things that go with momentous events," President Bush has said. "The Germans have already sent a piece of the Berlin Wall. In addition we will have all the papers documenting what led up to the U.S. role in unification."[3]

The George Bush School of Government and Public Service

The George Bush School of Government and Public Service will be a key component of the Library Center. Offering a master of public administration degree, it will emphasize the acquisition of analytical skills, the character of leadership, and management techniques for public service. It is the hope of President and Mrs. Bush that inclusion of academic programs in the

Seated at his computer, President Bush composed memos and thank you notes for which he
became famous within the White House.

complex will provide students with opportunities to visit the library regular-
ly and to draw upon its resources. It is also anticipated that students will
have some personal contact with President and Mrs. Bush when they are in
residence at the Center.

The Center for Presidential Studies

The Center for Presidential Studies will be adjacent to the presidential library and will be a leading center in the United States on the American presidency. Already established, this Center conducts research on presidential
decision making, world leadership, and relations with Congress and the
public. Its findings are disseminated to other scholars, government officials,

and the general public through numerous publications, symposia, lectures, and television programs.

The Center for Public Leadership Studies

In association with the Bush School of Government, the Center for Public Leadership Studies will draw on appropriate resources to enhance citizens' understanding of leadership and to encourage its development. Research findings will be disseminated in symposia, workshops, and lectures by and for public leaders.

Regarding public service, President Bush has said:

I hope my life has demonstrated a commitment to public service that was inculcated into me very early on by my father, and into him by his father. We believe in this concept of public service. So in this new school ... this new academic enterprise ... we can highlight what motivated people to be in public service ... how you set the highest standards for public service. I am personally very interested in that.[4]

The George Bush Presidential Library Center will open to the public in the spring of 1997. For additional information, write the George Bush Presidential Library Center, Texas A&M University, College Station, Texas 77843, or phone (409) 862-2251.

NOTES

1. For background information, see *George Bush Presidential Library Center at Texas A&M University,* Texas A&M University, Office of University Relations, 1994. See also *Biography of President George Bush,* George Bush Presidential Library Foundation, Texas A&M University, College Station, Texas, July 1, 1993.

2. *George Bush Presidential Library Center,* four-color brochure, George Bush Presidential Library Foundation, Texas A&M University, College Station, Texas, 1994, 4.

3. Ibid., 5.

4. Ibid., 3

Library Resources

Library Use, Resources, and Contacts

═══◄◉►═══

People interested in using the presidential libraries include teachers, journalists, students, attorneys, government officials, and university faculty. Their requests for information usually arrive by mail and telephone. On-site users are typically scholars doing research for publication or students preparing course papers.

Library research rooms are open Monday through Friday, except federal holidays. When preparing to do research at a presidential library, you should write or call the archival staff beforehand to find out whether the material you are interested in using is available. The staff will then advise you regarding the quantity and quality of the library's holdings on your topic. They may also send you a basic guide to that particular library as well as information regarding available grants, local accommodations, travel directions, and research regulations.

Individuals who have made arrangements to work on-site will be met and receive orientation from an archivist. Researchers are required to show personal identification and to complete a simple application for research.

Most of the documents stored within the presidential libraries are open to the general public. However, some of the documents in the newest libraries are still being processed. They may contain classified material or material that would be an unwarranted invasion of an individual's privacy if released. Circulation of still other documents may be limited by an agreement between the library and the material's donor.

THE RUTHERFORD B. HAYES PRESIDENTIAL CENTER
1337 Hayes Avenue, Fremont, Ohio 43420, (419) 332-2081

This library is a private facility and is not part of the federal government's system of presidential libraries. Unlike the other libraries listed here, it is open to the general public.

An open Reading Room contains Ohio county history books and atlases as well as out-of-state history books and genealogies. With the assistance of a librarian, additional holdings can be obtained from the closed stack area. The hours are 9:00 A.M. to 5:00 P.M., Monday through Saturday. The library is closed Sundays and holidays. Admission is free.

THE HERBERT HOOVER LIBRARY
P.O. Box 488, West Branch, Iowa 52358, (319) 643-5301

The library's holdings include the papers of Herbert Hoover and those of public figures such as Lewis Strauss, Gerald P. Nye, Felix Morley, Clark Mollenhoff, Robert E. Wood, Westbrook Pegler, and Laura Ingalls Wilder. More than 150 collections make this library an important center for the study of conservative journalistic thought, agricultural economics, famine relief, atomic energy, and governmental reorganization.

THE FRANKLIN D. ROOSEVELT LIBRARY
511 Albany Post Road, Hyde Park, New York 12538, (914) 229-8114

The library's holdings include Franklin D. Roosevelt's papers; the extensive papers of his wife, Eleanor Roosevelt; and those of more than one hundred friends and associates gathered during his lengthy political career as New York State senator (1910–1913), assistant secretary of the navy (1913–1920), unsuccessful vice presidential candidate (1920), two-term governor of New York (1929–1933), and president (1933–1945).

THE HARRY S. TRUMAN LIBRARY
U.S. Highway 24 and Delaware, Independence, Missouri 64050, (816) 833-1400

The library's holdings include the presidential papers of Harry S. Truman, several other collections of his papers documenting his life and career before and after the presidency, and more than 400 other manuscript collections related to his career. In addition, there are large collections of audiovisual materials; books, articles, and other printed items; oral history interviews; and museum objects.

THE DWIGHT D. EISENHOWER LIBRARY
Abilene, Kansas 67410, (913) 263-4751

The library's holdings include the documents of the Eisenhower presidency and military service, as well as manuscript materials of some 400 friends and associates from General Eisenhower's long career. The White House was the source of 11 million pages of manuscript materials, as well as thousands of photographs, sound recordings, books, and other materials.

The extensive audiovisual collection is significant because Eisenhower's administration was the first to be widely covered by television. The library contains 2,298 audio tapes and discs, 210,000 still films, and 536 motion films. In addition, it has seventy-five 35-millimeter motion picture films.

THE JOHN FITZGERALD KENNEDY LIBRARY
Columbia Point, Boston, Massachusetts 02125, (617) 929-4523

The library's holdings include the public and private papers of John F. Kennedy (8.4 million pages) and of members of the Kennedy family. Also available are the papers of many men and women who played major roles in the second half of the twentieth century (34 million total manuscript pages). The library contains 180,000 still photographs, 6 million feet of film and videotape, 1,000 audio tapes, and 15,000 total objects. In addition, the library has virtually all the surviving manuscripts of Nobel Prize-winning author Ernest Hemingway, including his original drafts of *A Farewell to Arms* and *For Whom the Bell Tolls*.

THE LYNDON BAINES JOHNSON LIBRARY
2313 Red River Street, Austin, Texas 78705, (512) 482-5137

The library's holdings include approximately 40 million pages of manuscripts, an extensive audiovisual collection, and oral history interviews with more than 1,000 individuals. The papers of Lyndon B. Johnson, which form the core of the library's holdings, include the White House files of his presidency (1963–1969) and papers from his service as a U.S. representative (1937–1949), U.S. senator (1949–1961), and vice president (1961–1963).

In addition, the library contains the papers of family, friends, and associates of Lyndon B. Johnson and members of his presidential administration such as Drew Pearson, Ramsey Clark, John Gardner, Dean Rusk, and Wright Patman.

Library collections are described in *Historical Materials in the Lyndon Baines Johnson Library* (1988), a copy of which can be obtained by writing to the supervisory archivist.

THE RICHARD NIXON LIBRARY
18001 Yorba Linda Boulevard, Yorba Linda, California 92686, (714) 993-3393

This library is a private facility and is not part of the federal government's system of presidential libraries. Its holdings include manuscript and audiovisual materials from Richard Nixon's service as a U.S. representative (1947–1951), U.S. senator (1951–1953), and vice president (1953–1961).

In addition, the library contains papers covering Nixon's personal life and post-presidential years plus manuscripts of his published books. Supplementing this core collection are materials collected by those closely associated with Nixon's career and with the international and domestic issues with which he dealt.

THE GERALD R. FORD LIBRARY
1000 Beal Avenue, Ann Arbor, Michigan 48109-2114, (313) 741-2218

The library's holdings include nearly 20 million manuscript and audiovisual items, the majority dealing with President Ford's White House years (1974–1977). In addition, the library holds his congressional and vice presidential papers, Betty Ford's papers, files of more than one hundred White House advisors and assistants, and the personal papers of individuals such as Federal Reserve Board chairman Arthur Burns and science advisor H. Guyford Stever.

Library collections are described in the *Guide to Historical Materials in the Gerald R. Ford Library* (1994), a free copy of which can be obtained by contacting the library. Prospective researchers may borrow finding aids to individual collections, obtain assessments of the quantity and quality of holdings, and request searches of the PRESNET collection description database to obtain lists of folders related to specific topics.

THE JIMMY CARTER LIBRARY
One Copenhill Avenue, Atlanta, Georgia 30307, (404) 331-0296

The library's holdings include the White House materials of President and Mrs. Carter and their staff. Other collections that further illumine that period of history have been added to the holdings, and new materials are acquired periodically. The library actively solicits material from the Carters' political and close personal friends, material of similar figures of secondary importance when they document significant aspects of the Carter administration, and material from President Carter's family.

THE RONALD REAGAN LIBRARY
40 Presidential Drive, Simi Valley, California 93065, (805) 522-8444

The Ronald Reagan Presidential Collection is the first presidential collection to be administered under the Presidential Records Act of 1978. This Act directs the archivist of the United States to take immediate custody of presidential documents when the president leaves office and to place them in a federal repository or presidential library, where they become the property of the United States.

The library's holdings include a complete collection of offcial records from the White House, numerous personal papers donated by President and Mrs. Reagan, and the official papers of many members of the Reagan Cabinet—a total of 47 million documents. In addition, still photographs, videotapes, motion picture film, and audio tapes are in storage. Many items from an extensive White House Gift Collection are also stored here.

The Ronald Reagan Center for Public Affairs is part of the library's mission. It was created to augment the study and appreciation of public policy.

THE GEORGE BUSH LIBRARY
Texas A&M University, College Station, Texas 77843

The George Bush Library is under construction and is scheduled to open to the public in spring 1997. The library's holdings will include a complete collection of official records from the Bush White House and numerous personal papers from his presidency, his career in the UN, China, and the CIA, and as vice president and world leader.

For additional information, write to the address above or phone (409) 862–2251.

Presidential Bibliography

Suggested readings on each president are listed below.

Rutherford B. Hayes

Barnard, Harry. *Rutherford B. Hayes and His America.* New York: Russell and Russell, 1967.

Eckenrode, H. J. *Rutherford B. Hayes: Statesman of Reunion.* New York: Dodd, Mead, 1930.

Hoogenboom, Ari. *The Presidency of Rutherford B. Hayes.* Lawrence: University Press of Kansas, 1988.

———— *Rutherford B. Hayes: Warrior and President.* Lawrence: University Press of Kansas, 1995.

McPherson, James M. "Coercion or Conciliation? Abolitionists Debate President Hayes's Southern Policy." *New England Quarterly* 39 (1966).

Williams, Charles Richard. *The Life of Rutherford Birchard Hayes: Nineteenth President of the United States.* 2 vols. Columbus: Ohio State Archaeological and Historical Society, 1928.

Williams, T. Harry, ed. *Hayes: Diary of a President 1875–1881.* New York: McKay, 1964.

Herbert Hoover

Burner, David. *Herbert Hoover: A Public Life.* New York: Knopf, 1979.

Hawley, Ellis W., et al. *Herbert Hoover and the Historians.* West Branch, Iowa: Hoover Library Association, 1986.

Hilton, Suzanne. *The World of Young Herbert Hoover.* New York: Walker, 1987.

Hoover, Herbert. *American Individualism and the Challenge to Liberty.* West Branch, Iowa: Hoover Library Association, 1989.

———— *Fishing for Fun and to Wash Your Soul.* West Branch, Iowa: Hoover Library Association, 1990.

——— *On Growing Up: Letters from and to American Children (1962)*. West Branch, Iowa: Hoover Library Association, 1990.

——— *The Ordeal of Woodrow Wilson (1958)*. Baltimore, Md.: Woodrow Wilson Center Press, 1992.

Mayer, Dale C., ed. *Lou Henry Hoover: Essays on a Busy Life*. Worland, Wyo.: High Plains Publishing, 1993.

Nash, George. *Life of Herbert Hoover the Engineer, 1874–1914*. New York: Norton, 1983.

——— *Life of Herbert Hoover the Humanitarian, 1914–1917*. New York: Norton, 1988.

Public Papers of the Presidents of the United States: Herbert Hoover, 4 vols.: 1929, 1930, 1931, 1932–1933. Washington, D.C.: National Archives and Records Administration, 1974 to 1978.

Smith, Richard Norton. *An Uncommon Man: The Triumph of Herbert Hoover*. Worland, Wyo.: High Plains Publishing, 1990.

Walch, Timothy, and Dwight M. Miller, eds. *Herbert Hoover and Harry S. Truman: A Documentary History*. Worland, Wyo.: High Plains Publishing, 1992.

Wilson, Joan Hoff. *Herbert Hoover: Forgotten Progressive*. Prospect Heights, Ill.: Waveland Press, 1992.

Franklin D. Roosevelt

Alsop, Joseph. *FDR: Centenary Remembrance*. New York: Viking, 1982.

Dallek, Robert. *Franklin D. Roosevelt, His Life and Times: An Encyclopedic View*. Boston: G. K. Hall, 1985.

Davis, Kenneth S. *FDR: The Beckoning of Destiny, 1882–1928*. New York: Putnam, 1973.

———. *FDR: The New York Years, 1928–1933*. New York: Random House, 1985.

———. *FDR: The New Deal Years, 1933–1937*. New York: Random House, 1986.

———. *FDR: Into the Storm, 1937–1940: A History*. New York: Random House, 1993.

FDR, His Personal Letters, Early Years. New York: Duell, Sloan and Pearce, 1948.

FDR, His Personal Letters, 1905–1928. New York: Duell, Sloan and Pearce, 1948.

FDR, His Personal Letters, 1928–1945, 2 vols. New York: Duell, Sloan and Pearce, 1950.

Larabee, Eric. *Commander in Chief*. New York: Harper and Row, 1987.

Lash, Joseph P. *Eleanor and Franklin: The Story of Their Relationship*. New York: Norton, 1972.

Ward, Geoffrey C. *Before the Trumpet: Young Franklin Roosevelt, 1882–1905*. New York: Harper and Row, 1985.

———. *A First Class Temperament: The Emergence of Franklin Roosevelt*. New York: Harper and Row, 1989.

Harry S. Truman

Acheson, Dean. *Present at the Creation: My Years in the State Department*. New York: Norton, 1959.

Donovan, Robert J. *Conflict and Crisis: The Presidency of Harry S. Truman, 1945–1948*. New York: Norton, 1977.

———. *Tumultuous Years: The Presidency of Harry S. Truman, 1949–1953*. New York: Norton, 1982.

Ferrell, Robert H., ed. *Dear Bess: The Letters from Harry to Bess Truman, 1910–1959*. New York: Harper and Row, 1983.

———, ed. *Off the Record: The Private Papers of Harry S. Truman*. New York: Harper and Row, 1980.

Kirkendall, Richard S., ed. *The Harry S. Truman Encyclopedia*. Boston: G.K. Hall, 1989.

McCullough, David. *Truman*. New York: Simon and Schuster, 1992.

Public Papers of the Presidents of the United States: Harry S. Truman. 8 vols. Washington, D.C.: U.S. Government Printing Office, 1961–1966.

Truman, Harry S. *Memoirs*. 2 vols. Garden City, New York: Doubleday, 1955–1956.

———. *Mr. Citizen*. New York: Bernard Geis and Associates, 1960.

Truman, Margaret. *Bess W. Truman*. New York: Macmillan, 1986.

———. *Harry S. Truman*. New York: William Morrow, 1973.

———, ed. *Where the Buck Stops: The Personal and Private Writings of Harry S. Truman*. New York: Warner Books, 1989.

Dwight D. Eisenhower

Ambrose, Stephen E. *Eisenhower: Soldier, General of the Army, President-Elect, 1890–1952*. vol. 1. New York: Simon and Schuster, 1983.

———. *Eisenhower: The President*. vol. 2. New York: Simon and Schuster, 1984.

Burk, Robert Fredrick. *Dwight D. Eisenhower: Hero and Politician*. Boston: Twayne Publishers, 1986.

Eisenhower, David. *Eisenhower at War: 1943–1945*. New York: Random House, 1986.

Eisenhower, Dwight D. *At Ease: Stories I Tell to Friends*. New York: Doubleday, 1967.

————. *Crusade in Europe.* New York: Doubleday, 1948.

————. *Ike's Letters to a Friend, 1948–1958,* edited by Robert Griffith. Lawrence: University Press of Kansas, 1984.

————. *Letters to Mamie,* edited, and with commentary, by John S. D. Eisenhower. New York: Doubleday, 1978.

————. *The Papers of Dwight David Eisenhower,* vols. 1–13. Baltimore, Md.: The John Hopkins University Press, 1970–1989.

Miller, Merle. *Ike the Soldier: As They Knew Him.* New York: Putnam, 1987.

Pach, Chester J., and Elmo R. Richardson. *The Presidency of Dwight D. Eisenhower.* Lawrence: University Press of Kansas, 1991.

John Fitzgerald Kennedy

Bernstein, Irving. *Promises Kept: John F. Kennedy's New Frontier.* New York: Oxford University Press, 1991.

Giglio, James N. *The Presidency of John F. Kennedy.* Lawrence: University Press of Kansas, 1992.

Goodwin, Doris Kearns. *The Fitzgeralds and the Kennedys.* New York: Simon and Schuster, 1986.

Hamilton, Nigel. *Reckless Youth.* New York: Random House, 1992.

Kennedy, Rose Fitzgerald. *Times to Remember.* New York: Doubleday, 1974.

O'Donnell, Kenneth P., and David F. Powers. *Johnny, We Hardly Knew Ye.* Boston: Little, Brown, 1972.

Parmet, Herbert S. *Jack: The Struggles of John F. Kennedy.* New York: Dial, 1980.

Reeves, Richard. *President Kennedy: Profile of Power.* New York: Simon and Schuster, 1993.

Salinger, Pierre. *With Kennedy.* New York: Doubleday, 1966.

Schlesinger, Arthur M., Jr. *A Thousand Days: John F. Kennedy in the White House.* Boston: Houghton Mifflin, 1965.

Sorensen, Theodore C. *Kennedy.* New York: Harper and Row, 1965.

Lyndon Baines Johnson

Bornet, Vaughn David. *The Presidency of Lyndon B. Johnson.* Lawrence: University Press of Kansas, 1983.

Califano, Joseph A. *The Triumph and Tragedy of Lyndon Johnson: The White House Years.* New York: Simon and Schuster, 1991.

Caro, Robert A. *The Years of Lyndon Johnson: The Path to Power.* Vol. 1. New York: Knopf, 1982.

————. *The Years of Lyndon Johnson: Means of Ascent.* Vol. 2. New York: Knopf, 1990.

Dallek, Robert. *Lone Star Rising: Lyndon Johnson and His Times, 1908–1960.* New York: Oxford University Press, 1991.

Kearns, Doris. *Lyndon Johnson and the American Dream.* New York: Harper and Row, 1976.

Middleton, Harry. *LBJ: The White House Years.* New York: Abrams, 1990.

Reedy, George. *Lyndon B. Johnson, A Memoir.* New York: Andrews and McMeel, 1982.

Rulon, Philip Reed. *The Compassionate Samaritan: The Life of Lyndon Baines Johnson.* Chicago: Nelson-Hall, 1981.

Valenti, Jack. *A Very Human President.* New York: Norton, 1975.

Richard Nixon

Aitken, Jonathan. *Nixon: A Life.* Washington, D.C.: Regnery, 1993.

Ambrose, Stephen E. *Nixon: The Education of a Politician, 1913–1962.* New York: Simon and Schuster, 1987.

————. *Nixon: The Triumph of a Politician, 1962–1972.* New York: Simon and Schuster, 1989.

————. *Nixon: Ruin & Recovery, 1973–1990.* New York: Simon and Schuster, 1991.

Eisenhower, Julie N. *Pat Nixon: The Untold Story.* New York: Simon and Schuster, 1986.

Larsen, Rebecca. *Richard Nixon: The Rise and Fall of a President.* New York: Franklin Watts, 1991.

McGinniss, Joe. *The Selling of the President.* New York: Viking Penguin, 1988.

Morris, Roger. *Richard Milhous Nixon: The Rise of an American Politician.* New York: Holt, 1990.

Nixon, Richard. *In the Arena.* New York: Simon and Schuster, 1990.

————. *Leaders.* (Richard Nixon Library), 1990. (Touchstone Books).

————. *RN: Memoirs of Richard Nixon.* (Richard Nixon Library), 1990. (Touchstone Books).

————. *Six Crises.* New York: Simon and Schuster, 1990.

Safire, William. *Before the Fall: An Inside View of the Pre-Watergate White House.* New York: Da Capo, 1988.

Woodward, Bob, and Carl Bernstein. *Final Days.* Beaverton, Ore.: Touchstone, 1994.

Gerald R. Ford

Cannon, James. *Time and Chance: Gerald Ford's Appointment with History.* New York: HarperCollins, 1993.

Ford, Betty. *The Times of My Life.* New York: Harper and Row, 1978.

Ford, Gerald R. *A Time to Heal: The Autobiography of Gerald R. Ford.* New York: Harper and Row, 1979.

Hartmann, Robert T. *Palace Politics: An Insider's Account of the Ford Years.* New York: McGraw-Hill, 1980.

Hersey, John. *The President: A Minute-by-Minute Account of a Week in the Life of Gerald Ford.* New York: Knopf, 1975.

LeRoy, David. *Gerald Ford—Untold Story.* Arlington, Va.: R.W. Beatty, 1974.

Mollenhoff, Clark R. *The Man Who Pardoned Nixon.* New York: St. Martin's Press, 1976.

Political Profiles: The Nixon-Ford Years. New York: Facts on File, 1979.

Schapsmeier, Edward L., and Frederick M. Schapsmeier. *Gerald R. Ford's Date with Destiny: A Political Biography.* New York: Lang, 1989.

terHorst, Jerald F. *Gerald Ford and the Future of the Presidency.* New York: Third Press, 1974.

Weidenfeld, Sheila Rabb. *First Lady's Lady: With the Fords at the White House.* New York: Putnam, 1979.

Jimmy Carter

Bishop, George F., Robert G. Meadow, and Marilyn Jackson-Beeck, eds. *The Presidential Debates.* New York: Praeger, 1978.

Califano, Joseph A., Jr. *Governing America.* New York: Simon and Schuster, 1981.

Callahan, Dorothy. *Jimmy: The Story of the Young Jimmy Carter.* Garden City, N.Y.: Doubleday, 1979.

Carter, Jimmy. *A Government As Good As Its People.* New York: Simon and Schuster, 1977.

———. *Keeping Faith: Memoir.* New York: Bantam Books, 1982.

———. *One Man, One Vote: A Candidate and a State Come of Age.* New York: Random House, 1992.

———. *Turning Point: A Candidate, a State, and a Nation Come of Age.* New York: Random House, 1993.

———. *Why Not the Best?* Nashville: Broadman Press, 1977.

Carter, Jimmy, and Rosalynn. *Everything to Gain.* New York: Random House, 1987.

Carter, Rosalynn. *First Lady from Plains.* New York: Fawcett, 1985.

Hyatt, Richard. *The Carters of Plains.* Huntsville, Ala.: Strode Publishers, 1977.

Lasky, Victor. *Jimmy Carter: The Man and the Myth.* New York: Richard Marek, 1979.

Miller, William Lee. *Yankee from Georgia.* New York: Time Books, 1978.

Norton, Howard. *Rosalynn.* Plainfield, N.J.: Logos International, 1977.

Norton, Howard, and Bob Slosser. *The Miracle of Jimmy Carter.* Plainfield, N.J.: Logos International, 1976.

The Presidential Campaign 1976. 3 vols. Washington, D.C.: U.S. Government Printing Office, 1978.

Public Papers of the Presidents of the United States: Jimmy Carter. Washington, D.C.: U.S. Government Printing Office, 1977.

Shogan, Robert. *Promises to Keep.* New York: Crowell, 1977.

Ronald Reagan

Cannon, Lou. *President Reagan: The Role of a Lifetime.* New York: Simon and Schuster, 1991.

Denton, Robert E., Jr. *The Primetime Presidency of Ronald Reagan: The Era of the Television Presidency.* Westport, Conn.: Greenwood, 1988.

Hogan, Joseph. *The Reagan Years: The Record in Presidential Leadership.* New York: St. Martin's Press, 1990.

Lees, J.D., et al. *Reagan's First Four Years: A New Beginning?* New York: St. Martin's Press, 1988.

Meese, Edwin, III. *With Reagan: The Inside Story.* Washington, D.C.: Regnery, 1992.

Mervin, David. *The Presidency and Ronald Reagan.* New York: Longman, 1990.

Public Papers of the Presidents of the United States: Ronald Reagan. 6 vols. Washington, D.C.: U.S. Government Printing Office, 1985–1990.

Reagan, Nancy, and William Novak. *My Turn.* New York: Dell, 1990.

Reagan, Ronald. *Ronald Reagan: An American Life.* New York: Simon and Schuster, 1990.

———. *Ronald Reagan Talks to America.* 2d rev. ed. Greenwich, Conn.: Devin, 1982.

Stockman, David A. *The Triumph of Politics: The Inside Story of the Reagan Revolution.* New York: Avon, 1987.

George Bush

Beschloss, Michael R., and Strobe Talbott. *At the Highest Levels: The Inside Story of the End of the Cold War.* Boston: Little, Brown, 1994.

Bush, George, with Victor Gold. *Looking Forward: The George Bush Story.* Garden City, N.Y.: Doubleday, 1987.

Bush, George, with Doug Wead. *Man of Integrity.* Eugene, Ore.: Harvest House, 1988.

Green, Fitzhugh. *George Bush: An Intimate Portrait.* New York: Hippocrene Books, 1990.

Hyams, Joe. *Flight of the Avenger: George Bush at War.* San Diego: Harcourt Brace Jovanovich, 1991.

Smith, Jean Edward. *George Bush's War.* New York: Holt, 1992.

Sufrin, Mark. *George Bush: The Story of the Forty-first President of the United States.* New York: Delacorte Press, 1989.

Tiefer, Charles. *The Semi-Sovereign Presidency: The Bush Administration's Strategy for Governing Congress.* Boulder: Westview Press, 1994.

Woodward, Bob. *The Commanders.* New York: Simon and Schuster, 1991.

Suggested readings on presidential libraries are listed below.

Geselbracht, Raymond. "The Four Eras in the History of Presidential Papers." *Prologue: Quarterly of the National Archives* (Spring 1983): 37–42.

Mackaman, Frank. "Human Drama: Presidential Museums Tell the Story." *Prologue: Quarterly of the National Archives* (Summer 1989): 135–145.

McCoy, Donald. *The National Archives: America's Ministry of Documents, 1934–1968.* Chapel Hill: University of North Carolina Press, 1978.

Schick, Frank. *Records of the Presidency: Presidential Papers and Libraries from Washington to Reagan.* Phoenix, Ariz.: Oryx Press, 1989.

U.S., National Archives and Records Administration, *Annual Report* (various years).

Veit, Fritz. *Presidential Libraries and Collections.* Westport, Conn.: Greenwood Press, 1987.

Index

INDEX

INDEX

INDEX

Credits

Introduction: Wide World/Associated Press, 2.

Chapter 1: All photos courtesy of the Rutherford B. Hayes Presidential Center.

Chapter 2: Herbert Hoover Library, 21, 22, 25, 27. Stock Montage, 18.

Chapter 3: Franklin D. Roosevelt Library, 30, 32, 33, 34, 42. National Archives, 35, 36. National Park Service, 31, 39, 43.

Chapter 4: Harry S. Truman Library, 45, 47, 49, 51, 52. Library of Congress, 53. UPI/Bettmann, 55.

Chapter 5: All photos courtesy Dwight D. Eisenhower Library.

Chapter 6: John F. Kennedy Library, 73, 75, 78, 81, 83, 84. Peter Vanderwalker/John F. Kennedy Library Foundation, 77, 82.

Chapter 7: Wide World/Associated Press, 94. All other photos, LBJ Library Collection.

Chapter 8: Courtesy of the White House, 100, 107. Richard Nixon Library, 102, 103, 114. Nixon Project/National Archives, 113. UPI/Bettmann, 109, 110.

Chapter 9: Congressional Quarterly, 121. All other photos, Gerald R. Ford Library.

Chapter 10: Congressional Quarterly, 132. All other photos, Jimmy Carter Library.

Chapter 11: National Archives, 146. Courtesy of the Ronald Reagan Presidential Library, 139 (top), 144. White House, 137, 139 (bottom), 147. Wide World/Associated Press, 142, 145.

Chapter 12: Courtesy of the Bush Presidential Materials Project, 149, 153. Courtesy of Texas A&M University, Office of University Relations, 151. White House, 152.

ABOUT THE AUTHOR

Pat Hyland is a writer who lives in Springfield, Virginia. She is a regular contributor to many publications in the Washington, D.C., metropolitan area.

ABOUT THE BOOK

Presidential Libraries and Museums was designed and typeset in QuarkXPress on a MacIntosh by Kachergis Book Design, Pittsboro, North Carolina. The typeface, Adobe Minion, was designed by Robert Slimbach and reflects the classical typography of the late Renaissance. *Presidential Libraries and Museums* was printed on seventy-pound Sterling Litho matte and bound by Braun Brumfield, Inc., Ann Arbor, Michigan.

Date Due

MAR 2 5 1997			
MAY 5 1998			
NOV 0 5 2008			

BRODART, CO.   Cat. No. 23-233-003   Printed in U.S.A.